GENERATING TRACES IN THE HISTORY
OF THE WORLD

Generating Traces in the History of the World

New Traces of the Christian Experience

Luigi Giussani
Stefano Alberto, Javier Prades

Translated by
Patrick Stevenson

McGill-Queen's University Press
Montreal & Kingston • London • Chicago

© McGill-Queen's University Press 2010
ISBN 978-0-7735-3767-5 (cloth)
ISBN 978-0-7735-3768-2 (paper)
ISBN 978-0-2280-0213-0 (ePDF)
ISBN 978-0-7735-8160-9 (ePUB)

Legal deposit third quarter 2010
Bibliothèque nationale du Québec

Revised by Damian Bacich

Reprinted 2019

This book is a translation of *Generare tracce nella storia del mondo*.
© Fraternità di Comunione e Liberazione.

Printed in Canada on acid-free paper that is 100% ancient forest free
(100% post-consumer recycled), processed chlorine free

Funded by the Government of Canada   Financé par le gouvernement du Canada   Canada Council for the Arts   Conseil des arts du Canada

We acknowledge the support of the Canada Council for the Arts.

Nous remercions le Conseil des arts du Canada de son soutien.

Library and Archives Canada Cataloguing in Publication

Giussani, Luigi
    Generating traces in the history of the world: new traces of the
    Christian experience / Luigi Giussani, Stefano Alberto, Javier Prades;
    translated by Patrick Stevenson

    Translation of: Generare tracce nella storia del mondo: nuove tracce
    d'esperienza cristiana.

    Includes bibliographical references and index.
    ISBN 978-0-7735-3767-5 (bound). – ISBN 978-0-7735-3768-2 (pbk.)
    ISBN 978-0-2280-0213-0 (ePDF). – ISBN 978-0-7735-8160-9 (ePUB)

    1. Spiritual life – Catholic Church. 2. Jesus Christ. I. Alberto, Stefano
II. Prades, Javier, 1960– III. Stevenson, Patrick IV. Title.

BX2350.2.G57413 2010   24.8.4'82   C2010-903051-6

This book was typeset by Interscript in 10/13 Sabon.

Contents

Editors' Note

This volume contains the basic outlines of Luigi Giussani's reflections on Christian experience.

These texts, which vary both in nature and literary style, have been organized and edited so as to form an organic whole and a unified discourse. We have made every effort to remain faithful to the original texts, retaining Giussani's sometimes unusual phrasing and the use of masculine terms to include all humanity, as is the accepted form in Italian.

This volume marks an essential moment and summarizes the route travelled thus far; at the same time, it is offered to the reader as an occasion to know and to delve more deeply into the contents and traits of the Christian proposal made to the people of our times.

Introduction

"In the Simplicity of my Heart I have gladly given You everything"

Fr Luigi Giussani's testimony during the meeting of the Holy Father
John Paul II with the ecclesial movements and the new communities.
St Peter's Square, Rome, 30 May 1998

I shall try to say how an attitude was born in me – an attitude
that God was to bless, as He wished – and that I could not have
foreseen nor even wished for.

1) "What is man that you should keep him in mind, mortal man
that you care for him?" (Psalms 8:5). No question in life has
ever struck me like this one. There has been only one Man in the
world who could answer me, by asking another question: "What
would it profit a man if he gain the whole world, and then lose
himself? Or what could a man give in exchange for himself?"
(Matthew 16:26). I was never asked a question that took my
breath away so much as this question of Christ's! No woman
ever heard another voice speak of her son with such an original
tenderness and unquestionable valuing of the fruit of her womb,
with such a wholly positive affirmation of its destiny; only the
voice of the Jew Jesus of Nazareth. And more than that, no man
can feel his own dignity and absolute value affirmed far beyond
all his achievements. No one in the world has ever been able to
speak like this!

Only Christ takes my humanity so completely to heart. This is
the wonder expressed by Dionysius the Areopagite (5th century):

"Who could ever speak to us of the love that Christ has for man, overflowing with peace?" I've been repeating these words to myself for more than fifty years!

This is why *Redemptor Hominis* appeared on our horizon like a beam of light in the thick darkness covering the earth of present-day man, with all his confused questions. Thank you, Your Holiness.

It was a simplicity of heart that made me feel and recognize Christ as exceptional, with that certain promptness that marks the unassailable and indestructible evidence of factors and moments of reality, which, on entering the horizon of our person, pierce us to the heart.

So the acknowledgment of who Christ is in our lives invades the whole of our awareness of living: "I am the Way, the Truth and the Life" (John 14:6).

"Domine Deus, in simplicitate cordis mei laetus obtuli universa" ("Lord God, in the simplicity of my heart I have gladly given You everything"), says a prayer of the Ambrosian Liturgy; what shows that this acknowledgement is true is the fact that life has an ultimate, tenacious capacity for gladness.

2) How can this gladness, which is the human glory of Christ, and which fills my heart and my voice in some moments, be found to be true and reasonable to today's man?

Because that Man, the Jew Jesus of Nazareth, died for us and rose again. That Risen Man is the Reality on which all the positivity of every man's existence depends.

Every earthly experience lived in the Spirit of Jesus, Risen from the dead, blossoms in Eternity. This blossoming will not bloom only at the end of time; it has already begun on the dawn of Easter. Easter is the beginning of this journey to the eternal Truth of everything, a journey that is therefore already within man's history.

For Christ, as the Word of God made flesh, makes Himself present as the Risen one in every period of time, throughout the whole of history, in order to reach from Easter morning to the end of this time, the end of this world. The Spirit of Jesus, that is to say of the Word made flesh, becomes an experience possible for ordinary man, in His power to redeem the whole existence of each person and human history, in the radical change that He produces in the one who encounters Him, and, like John and Andrew, follows Him.

Thus for me the grace of Jesus, insofar as I have been able to adhere to the encounter with Him and communicate Him to the brothers in God's Church, has become the experience of a faith that in the Holy Church, that is to say the Christian People, revealed itself as a call and a desire to feed a new Israel of God: "*Populum Tuum vidi, cum ingenti gaudio, Tibi offerre donare*" ("With great joy, I saw your People, acknowledging existence as an offering to You"), continues the liturgical prayer.

So it was that I saw a people taking shape, in the name of Christ. Everything in me became truly more religious, with my awareness striving to discover that "God is all in all" (1 Corinthians 15:28). In this people gladness was becoming "*ingenti gaudio*", that is to say the decisive factor of one's own history as ultimate positivity and therefore as joy.

What could have seemed at most to be an individual experience was becoming a protagonist in history, and so an instrument of the mission of the one People of God.

This now is the foundation of the search for an expressed unity among us.

3) That precious text of the Ambrosian Liturgy concludes with these words: "*Domine Deus, custodi hanc voluntatem cordis eorum*" ("Lord God, keep safe this attitude of their heart").

Infidelity always arises in our hearts even before the most beautiful and true things; the infidelity in which, before God's humanity and man's original simplicity, man can fall short, out of weakness and worldly preconception, like Judas and Peter. Even this personal experience of infidelity that always happens, revealing the imperfection of every human action, makes the memory of Christ more urgent.

The desperate cry of Pastor Brand in Ibsen's play of the same name, ("Answer me, O God, in the hour in which death is swallowing me up: is the whole of man's will not enough to achieve even a part of salvation?") is answered by the humble positivity of St Theresa of the Child Jesus who writes, "When I am charitable it is only Jesus who is acting in me."

All this means that man's freedom, which the Mystery always involves, has *prayer* as its supreme, unassailable expressive form. This is why freedom, according to the whole of its true nature, posits itself as an entreaty to adhere to Being, therefore to Christ. Even in man's incapacity, in man's great weakness, affection for Christ is destined to last.

In this sense Christ, Light and Strength for every one of His followers, is the adequate reflection of that word with which the Mystery appears in its ultimate relationship with the creature, as *mercy*: *Dives in Misericordia*. The mystery of mercy shatters any image of complacency or despair; even the feeling of forgiveness lies within this mystery of Christ.

This is the ultimate embrace of the Mystery, against which man – even the most distant, the most perverse or the most obscured, the most in the dark – cannot oppose anything, can make no objection. He can abandon it, but in so doing he abandons himself and his own good. The Mystery as mercy remains the last word even on all the awful possibilities of history.

For this reason existence expresses itself, as ultimate ideal, in *begging*. The real protagonist of history is the beggar: Christ who begs for man's heart, and man's heart that begs for Christ.

GENERATING TRACES IN THE HISTORY OF THE WORLD

I

The Christian Event as an Encounter

I ANDREW AND JOHN

Christianity is the announcement that God became a man, born of a woman, in a fixed place and at a fixed time. The Mystery that lies at the root of all things decided to make Himself known to man.[1] It is a fact that happened in history, the breaking into time and into space of an exceptional human Presence. God made Himself known by revealing Himself, by taking the initiative of becoming a factor in human experience, in an instant that was decisive for the whole life of the world.

"After forty days of fasting and contemplation He came back to the place of baptism. He knew already for what encounter. "The Lamb of God!" says the prophet as he sees Him coming (surely in a whisper). This time two of John's disciples were with Him. They looked at Jesus, and that look was enough: they followed Him to the place where He lived. One of the two was Andrew, Simon's brother; the other John, the son of Zebedee: "Jesus looked at him and loved him." What is written about the rich young man, who would go away sad, is taken for granted here. What did Jesus do to keep them there? "As He saw they were following Him, He said to them, 'What are you looking for?' and they answered, 'Rabbi, where do you live?' He said, 'Come and see.' They went and saw where He was living and stayed with Him that day. It was about the tenth hour."[2]

This is how François Mauriac, in his *Life of Jesus*, recounts the first emergence of that presence as a "problem" that affects history for all time.

Chapter 1 of St John's Gospel is the first page of literature to speak of this. In addition to the explicit announcement – "The Word was made flesh,"[3] that of which all reality is made has become man – it contains the memory of the first two men who followed Him. Years later, one of them set down in writing the impressions and the features of that first instant when the event occurred. He reads in his memory the notes that are still there.[4] The whole of St John's first chapter, after the Prologue (vv. 1-18), is a sequence of phrases that are really notes from memory. For memory does not have a law of uninterrupted continuity, like fiction; memory literally "takes notes": a note, a line, a point, so that one sentence covers many things, and the next sentence begins after many things that were not spelled out in the previous one. Things are inferred rather than actually said; only some are said, as reference points.

"The following day John was still there with two of his disciples. Fixing his eyes on Jesus, who was passing, he said ..."[5] Picture the scene. After one hundred and fifty years of waiting, the Hebrew people, who had always had prophets throughout a thousand years of its history, finally has another: John the Baptist. Other ancient writers speak of him, he is historically documented. So, at long last, came John, called "the Baptizer." The way he lived impressed everyone. From the Pharisees to the humblest peasant, they left their homes to go to listen to him, at least once. Everybody – rich and poor, tax collectors and Pharisees, friends and foes, from Galilee and from Judea – went to hear John[6] and to see the way he was living, on the far side of the Jordan, in a desert land, feeding on locusts and wild herbs. He always had a group of listeners around him. Among these people, *that day* were two who came for the first time. They came from the lake, which was rather far away, outside the area of built-up towns. They were two fishermen of Galilee. They felt out of place there, like two peasants going to town, and they were watching everything around them closely, especially the Baptist. With eyes and mouth wide open, they were watching him, paying close attention. Suddenly a young man, one of the group, who had joined the others in listening to the prophet, walked away on the path along the river leading north. Immediately John the Baptist focused his gaze on Him and cried out, "There is the Lamb of God, who takes away the sin of the world!"[7] People did not budge: they were used to hearing the prophet come out, now and again, with strange, meaningless phrases, unconnected and out of context. So most of those present took no notice. But those two were there for the first time, hanging on his every word, following his gaze with their eyes, and they noticed that as he was saying those words he had his eyes on that individual who was walking away. And they set off after Him. They followed Him from a distance, afraid and embarrassed, yet strangely, profoundly, obscurely, magnetically moved to curiosity. "Those two disciples, hearing him speak like that, followed Jesus. Jesus turned around, saw that they were following Him, and said, 'What are you seeking?' They answered, 'Rabbi, where do you live?' He said to them, 'Come and see.'"[8] "Come and see." This is *the* Christian formula, the Christian method. "They came and saw where he was staying; and they stayed with him that day, for it was about the tenth hour."[9]

The narrative specifies nothing else. The whole passage, even the next one, as we have said, is made up of notes: sentences end at a point that assumes that many things are already known. The time is indicated ("the tenth hour" is four p.m.), but nothing is said of when they arrived, nor of when they left. The narrative continues, "One of the two who had heard John the Baptist's words and had followed Him was called Andrew, he was Simon Peter's brother. He first met his brother Simon, who was coming back from the shore, either from fishing or from mending his nets, and told him, 'We have found the Messiah.'"[10] Nothing is added, nothing is quoted, nothing is documented; it is well known. These are notes about things everybody knows! Few pages can be read like these, so realistically and simply truthful, where no word is added to the essential that is fixed by memory. How could Andrew have told his brother, "We have found the

Messiah"? Jesus must have used this word when He had spoken
to them. It was a word in their dictionary, else it would have been
impossible for them to say and so suddenly to assert that He was
the Messiah.

It is obvious that after listening to that Man for hours, watching Him speak ("Who is He who is speaking like this? Who else
has ever spoken like this? Who has ever said these things? I've
never seen or heard anyone like him!"), a precise impression had
slowly formed in their heart: "If I don't believe this man, I'll not
believe anyone, I'll not believe my own eyes!" They did not spell
it out, perhaps they did not form the thought, but they certainly
felt it. That man must have affirmed, among other things, that
he was the Messiah, the One who was to come. He was so clear
in making this exceptional affirmation that they accepted it as
something simple, easy to understand. It was something simple!

"Andrew led Simon to Jesus. Jesus fixed His eyes on him and
said, 'You are Simon, the son of John. You will be called Cephas
(which means rock).'"[11] The Jews used to change someone's name
either to describe his character or to recall something that had
happened to him. Let us imagine Simon going with his brother,
full of curiosity and a little afraid, and looking at the Man to
whom he was being led. The Man is watching him from afar. Let's
picture the way Jesus was looking at him, piercing him to the very
marrow of his bones. Let's think of how He saw through his character, "You'll be called Rock." What an impression it must have
made, to feel looked at like that by someone, a total stranger, and
feel oneself understood in the depth of one's being.

"The following day Jesus had decided to leave for Galilee."[12]
This page is entirely made up of these short hints, of these points
where what had happened is taken for granted, as evident and
well known to everybody.

Exceptional and with a deep human sympathy

How could the first two, John and Andrew (Andrew was probably
married with children), have been won over at once and recognize
Him ("We have found the Messiah")? There is an apparent dis-

proportion between the extremely simple way it all happened and the certainty of the two. If this fact happened, then recognizing that Man, who that Man was, not in depth and detail, but in His unique and unparalleled ("divine") value, must have been easy. Why was it easy to recognize Him? Because He was *exceptional* beyond compare. They had come into contact with an exceptional Man, someone absolutely extraordinary, impossible to reduce to any analysis.

What does "exceptional" mean? When can something be defined as "exceptional"? When it corresponds adequately to the heart's original expectations, however confused and hazy one's aware-ness of it may be. Exceptional is, paradoxically, when what is most "natural" for us appears. And what is "natural" for us? That what we desire should come true. For nothing is more natural than the satisfaction of the ultimate and profound desire of our heart, noth-ing is more natural than the answer to the needs that lie at the root of our being, those needs for which we actually live and move. Our heart has an ultimate, imperious, deep-set need for fulfillment, for truth, beauty, goodness, love, final certitude, and happiness. So to come across an answer to these needs should be the most obvious and normal thing. Yet, on the contrary, this correspondence, which should be supremely normal, becomes supremely exceptional for us. To come face to face with something absolutely and profoundly natural, that is to say, something that corresponds to the needs of the heart that nature gives us, is therefore something absolutely exceptional. There is, as it were, a strange contradiction: what normally happens is never truly exceptional, because it does not respond adequately to the needs of our heart.

It is the exceptionality of the figure of Christ, then, that makes it easy to recognize Him. For John and Andrew, that Man cor-responded to the irresistible and undeniable needs of their heart in a way that was unimaginable. There was no one like that man. In the encounter with Him, they felt an unimagined, unimagin-able correspondence to the heart that they had never before ex-perienced. What an unprecedented astonishment He must have awoken in the two who first met Him, and later in Simon, Philip, and Nathanael!

Not only was it easy to recognize Him, it was very easy to live in a relationship with Him. It was enough to adhere to the bond He generated, a *deep sympathy*, like the dizzying, carnal bond a child has with his mother, which is sympathy in the deepest meaning of the term. A child can misbehave a thousand times a day with his mother, but God help you if you take him from her! Were he to understand the question "Do you love this woman?" imagine how he would shout "Yes!" The more he had misbehaved, the more he would shout, "Yes, I love her!" to reaffirm it. This is the logic of knowledge and morality that life with that Man made necessary: a profound sympathy. Learning from His exceptional nature was therefore an ultimate sympathy made manifest.

2 GOD'S METHOD

An event, not our thoughts·

The first chapter of St John's Gospel documents the very simple and profound manner in which Christianity emerged in history: the happening of a human event, the encounter with an exceptional presence. For John and Andrew, Christianity, i.e., the fulfillment of the Law, the fulfillment of the ancient promise in whose hope the faithful remnant of the Hebrew people (Anna the prophetess,[13] Simeon,[14] the shepherds,[15] all described in the first chapters of St Luke) had lived, the Messiah, the One who was to come and for whom the people were waiting, was a man standing right before their eyes. They had come across Him, they had followed Him, they had gone to His home and spent the whole afternoon there with Him, filled with astonishment, openmouthed, watching Him speak. And when, on their way back, they said, "We have found the Messiah," they were repeating with certainty words they had heard from Him. The fulfillment of the great biblical promise was a man right before their eyes. *Event*: No word in the dictionary reflects the way in which the "issue" became real, became flesh in time, better than the word "event." Christianity is an "event," something that was not there before and arose at a given point." Not that John and Andrew

said, "What happened to us is an event." It was clearly not necessary for them to specify what was happening to them by means
of a definition. It was happening!

Christianity is an event. There is no other word to indicate its
nature, neither the word *law*, nor the words *ideology*, *concept*,
or *plan*. Christianity is not a religious doctrine, a series of moral
laws or a collection of rites. Christianity is a fact, an event. All
the rest is a consequence. The word "event" is therefore crucial. It
indicates the method chosen and used by God to save man:[16] God
became man in the womb of a fifteen- to seventeen-year-old girl
named Mary, in "the womb ... where our desire did dwell,"[17] as
Dante says. The *manner* in which God entered into relationship
with us to save us is an *event*, not a thought or a religious senti-
ment.[18] It is a fact that took place in history, a fact that reveals
who God is and points out what God wants from man, what man
must do in his relationship with God. As a way of communicating
Himself to man, God could have chosen direct enlightenment, so
that each individual would have to follow what God suggested to
him in his thoughts and in his heart. This would have been by
no means an easier or safer road, since it would be constantly
exposed to the fluctuation of feelings and thoughts. But the way
God chose to save us is an event, not our thoughts![19]

For the salvation of man

Christianity is an event that man comes across, and in which
man discovers himself to be "of the same blood."[20] It is a fact
that reveals the self to itself. "When I encountered Christ I discovered myself to be a man"[21] said the Roman rhetor, Marius
Victorinus. To say that man is "saved" means he recognizes who
he is, he recognizes his destiny and knows how to direct his
steps towards it. As Albert Camus writes, "it is not by scruples
that man will become great. Greatness comes, if God so wants,
as a fine day."[22] It is an event – the breaking in of something
new – that gives rise to a process whereby the self begins to become aware of itself, aware of the destiny towards which it is
heading, aware of the journey it is making, of its rights, of the

duties it must respect, and of its entire makeup. The dynamic of an event, moreover, marks out the way of knowing in each new step it takes.[23] Without an "event," nothing new is known, no new element enters our awareness. The French critic Alain Finkielkraut, in an interview on the relevance of the poet Charles Péguy for today, states the following, "An event is something that breaks in from without, something unforeseen. And this is *the supreme method of cognition.* We need to give back to the event its ontological dimension of a *new beginning.* It is a breaking in of the new that breaks apart the mechanism, and that sets a process to motion."[24] To come to know is to come face-to-face with something new, something outside ourselves, not built by us, something that breaks the mechanism of the things already established, the definitions already given. Cesare Pavese says, "Something external has to intervene in order to change direction."[25] An event is therefore crucial for every "discovery," every type of knowledge.

Now, that Fact, the event of an exceptional human presence, posits itself as the method chosen by God to reveal man to himself, to awaken him to a definitive clarity regarding the factors that constitute him, to open him up to recognize his destiny and to sustain him on the journey towards it, and to make him into a subject suited to action that bears the meaning of the world within history. This event, then, is what sets in motion the process through which man becomes fully conscious of himself, of his entire physiognomy, and begins to say "I" with dignity.

God became an event in our daily existence, so that our "I" might recognize itself with clarity in its original factors and attain its destiny, be saved. So it was for Mary and Joseph. So it was for John and Andrew, who followed Jesus, taking their cue from John the Baptist. God was entering their lives as an event. Whether they always kept it in mind or at times forgot it, especially during the early days and months, the whole of their lives depended on that event. Insofar as an event is important, you cannot retreat from it. That is how it was with them. This is how it is today with us: an event can mark the beginning of a journey. The event can point to a *method for life.* It is, in any case, an experience to be had. This journey requires the engagement of the person who is struck by the event, and will eventually reveal the true meaning of what he or she has begun to glimpse: it is the development of a way of looking at things.[26]

3 WHAT AN EVENT IS

If man's salvation happens according to the method chosen by God (as we have seen for John and Andrew) and this method is that of an event, then we need to clarify this word further. What is the ontology of event? What consistency and meaning does it have?

Let us imagine an everyday situation. Two young people marry, and nine months later have a baby. Can we say that an event has happened? Yes. As much as they conceived it and waited for it, it is nevertheless evident that that child was not "fabricated" by them, from the very fact that they met, decided to become a couple and to marry. In this sense, we could say that the child came about "by chance."

Boethius, recalling Aristotle, defines chance as an effect greater than the sum of its known causes. He offers the example of a peasant who digs in his field and unearths a treasure.[27] The peasant meant to till his field; the last thing he was imagining was to find a treasure. He finds it by chance. It is an effect greater than the sum of the known causes. For the causes previously known to the peasant do not lead "necessarily" to the discovery. The phrase, "by digging a field I find a treasure" is therefore meaningless, without reason. Yet, once the treasure has been discovered, another order of causes comes to light: not only land to be tilled, but a rich man too, who, in a hurry to flee, buried that treasure. It is a new order of causes, as yet unknown, of which the peasant was unaware. We can then say that the phrase "by digging a field I find a treasure" is not rational according to the order of the known causes, but is perfectly rational according to an order of causes that we come to discover later. This is why, Boethius concludes, chance can be defined as an "unforeseeable event" *(inopinatum eventum)*.[28]

"Chance" refers to something "happening." The word *chance* expresses event in the way closest to everyday language, in the most common way. Chance indicates something unforeseen and unforeseeable, something that cannot be deduced from the analysis of its antecedents. The closest word to event, something that happens, is therefore the word chance. *Event* means "coming from" (*e-venio*). *Happening* means "coming about by chance," so event and happening refer more to chance than to necessity. They are words that verge on Mystery.

Even creation is an event; in fact, it is the first and fundamental event.[29] The dynamic of event describes every instant of life: the flower in the field "which the Father clothes better than Solomon" is an event; the bird that falls "and the heavenly Father knows it," is an event; "the hairs on your head are numbered," they are an event.[30] Even heaven and earth, which have existed for a million centuries, are an event: an event that still occurs as something new, since their explanation is inexhaustible. To glimpse something greater in the relationship with everything means that the relationship itself is event,[31] and if man does not look at the world as something given, as an event, starting from the gesture of God which gives it to him now, it loses all its attraction, surprise, and moral appeal; in other words, the appeal to adhere to the order and the destiny of things.

So, a child that is born is an event, the creation of the world is an event: all realities have as their common denominator the fact that man cannot ultimately explain them or give them an exhaustive definition. An event then can be defined as the emergence into experience of something that cannot be analyzed in all its factors, something that contains a vanishing point in the direction of Mystery and that retains the reference to an unknown, to the point that, as we have said, we can even call it "chance."

At this stage we can define the ontology of an event as the transparency of the real that emerges into experience insofar as it derives from the Mystery – something we cannot possess or dominate. In this sense, we add, an event is by its nature a novelty, something new. With an event, something new enters our life: something unforeseen, not defined beforehand, not willed by us as the outcome of a plan to be realized, always "vanishing" into the unforeseeable; or rather, as much "vanishing" into the unforeseeable before it happens, as it is precise, concrete, visible, tangible, embraceable, when it does happen. When it happens, an event is something that is there; it can be experienced, it is visible and tangible. In this sense, the mystery of Incarnation is an Event that, although man did not and could not foresee or imagine it, reveals itself to be supremely "worthwhile"; that is, correspondent to the most particular needs of his nature.

If we do not understand and use the term "event," we shall not even understand Christianity, which will thus be immediately reduced to a word, to a work of man, the outcome of human activity. So, an event indicates the contingent, the apparent, the experiential, because it is apparent, as something born from Mystery, as a "datum," not in the scientific sense of "data," but in the profound and original Latin meaning of the word: *datum*, something that is given. An event is therefore a fact that surfaces within experience and reveals the Mystery that constitutes it.

4 A DIFFICULTY IN UNDERSTANDING: MAN CANNOT MAINTAIN THE ORIGINAL POSITION

Yet "event" is the word that the modern mentality, and therefore each one of us, finds hardest to understand and to accept. In the whole of Christian language, nothing is perceived with greater resistance (save by those who are pure in heart and childlike in soul) than the word "event." By "event" we mean to identify both an ideal position (Christ is the ideal of life) and a doctrinal position (Christ is the consistency of everything).[32] The hardest thing to accept is that it is an event that awakens us to ourselves, to the truth of our life, to our own destiny, to hope, to morality.

The word "event" indicates a place where the reality that can be experienced and Mystery "coincide." An event is something new that enters into the experience that a person is having. Inasmuch as it enters experience, it is the object of reason, and therefore it is rational to affirm it; inasmuch as it is something

new, it implies that reason should open to what is beyond: it is
the appearing of the Mystery. "Event" indicates the "coincid-
ing" of reality with Mystery, of normal experience with Mystery.
Recognizing reality as deriving from the Mystery should be familiar to reason, because precisely in recognizing what is real, just
as it is, as God wanted it to be, rather than reduced, flattened out,
without depth, we find a correspondence with the needs of our
heart, and our innate capacity for reason and affectivity is fully
realized. For reason, owing to its own very original dynamic,
cannot fulfill itself unless it recognizes that reality is rooted in
Mystery. Human reason reaches its apex, and so is truly reason,
when it recognizes things for what they are, and things as they
are proceed from an Other. What intensity of life is promised to
those who grasp, instant by instant, the relationship of everything with the origin! Each instant enjoys a definitive relationship with the Mystery, and so nothing is lost: this is what we
exist for, and this is our happiness.

   Yet there is a wound in man's heart that distorts something inside him and he cannot, by his own strength, remain in truth. He
fixes his attention and his desire on particular and limited things.
The original plan, that for which man is created, was altered by
the arbitrary use of freedom. Thus men tend towards a particular, which, when detached from the whole, is identified as life's
aim. The experience we live every day is that men tend to identify
the totality of life with something partial and limited. Escaping
this partiality is not in our hands. None of us can, alone, recover
a true way of looking at reality.[33]

5   THE RELIGIOUS SENSE AND FAITH

The incomprehension and hostility of the modern mentality towards the word *event* are reflected in the way the concept of
"faith" is reduced. The modern mentality confuses "religious
sense" with "faith" by a prejudiced refusal to consider the method chosen by God for responding to man's need for total meaning: a Fact in time and space. Let's therefore distinguish the two
terms, according to their respective dynamics.

In each human self that observes itself in action within its living and active present, the *religious sense* identifies the ultimate nature of its existential experience; that is, the level of those ineradicable desires, those irreducible needs that each man discovers as constituting his being.[34] These ultimate factors, which are the structure of man's life, have the breadth of the relationship with infinity: they are greater than anything we can imagine because they are infinite in their capacity for relationship. They spring forth from the deep well where our self is born and, in their functioning, from the surface of appearances they reach back to the deep well of their origin, of Being.

The religious sense is nothing other than the demand for totality that constitutes our reason, present in every action, since man's every action is provoked by a need. Since this need is dictated by an aspect of the demands of our heart, the true, exhaustive answer is incommensurable. So, the religious sense is reason as awareness of reality as a whole.[35] Religious sense and reason are therefore the same thing. Man's religious sense coincides with reason in its profound aspect of unflagging striving towards the ultimate meaning of reality.[36] It appears therefore as the most authentic application of the term reason; it indicates its boundless thrust as a thirst for totality. This boundless thrust towards infinity is what drives reason to take interest in all the factors of reality. The proper object of this thrust is the ultimate "why" of the present, the ultimate origin of the particular and of oneself. All "religious experience," then, is born of the need for total meaning, which manifests itself as the lived intuition of the Mystery, since it is the incommensurable answer to this need. Faced with this enigmatic incommensurability, man seeks, as it were, a ground more in proportion with himself upon which to build the "site" of his relationship with the Mystery.[37] Thus "religions" are born. They represent the numerous expressions of that creative effort that man has always made to imagine his relationship with the Mystery.[38]

To the modern man, "faith" would generically be nothing more than an aspect of religious experience, a kind of feeling with which he could live out the restless search for his origin and his destiny, which is precisely the most appealing element of every "religion." All modern consciousness is bent on tearing the hypothesis of Christian faith away from man, and on reducing faith to the dynamic of the religious sense and to the concept of religious experience. Unfortunately this confusion also penetrates the mentality of Christian people.

The dynamic of *faith*, as it emerges within Christian revelation, is quite different. Here it is no longer our reason that explains, but our reason that opens up – thus perceiving the fulfillment of its dynamic – to God's self-revelation. In this way the divine Mystery communicates its nature, its "thoughts" and "ways," manifesting itself in time and space. While religious experience springs from the need for meaning that is awakened by the impact with the real, faith is the recognition of an exceptional Presence that corresponds totally to our destiny, and the adherence to this Presence. Faith means to recognize that what a historical Presence says of itself is true.

Christian faith is the memory of a historical fact: a Man said something about Himself that others accepted as true, and that I, too, accept because of the exceptional way in which that fact still reaches me. Jesus is a man who said, "I am the way, the truth and the life."[39] It is a Fact that happened in history: a child, born of woman, registered in the Bethlehem birth register,[40] who, once He had grown up, announced He was God: "The Father and I are one."[41] Paying attention to what that Man did and said to the point of saying, "I believe in this Man," adhering to His Presence, and affirming what He said as the truth: this is faith. Faith is an act of reason moved by the exceptional nature of a Presence that brings man to say, "This man who is speaking is truthful. He is not lying, I accept what He says." Let us imagine what a challenge the claim of faith represents for the modern mentality: that a man exists, a man to whom I can say You, who says, "Without me you can do nothing";[42] that a Man exists who is God. We never measure ourselves completely against this claim. Today, neither normal people nor the greatest philosophers tackle this problem any longer, or if they do at all, it is to consolidate the negative preconception inherited from the prevailing mentality.

In other words, the answer to the Christian problem "Who is Jesus?" is deduced from pre-constituted conceptions about man and the world. Yet Jesus's answer is, "Look at my works"; in other words, "Look at me," which is the same thing.[43] Yet people don't look Him in the face, they eliminate Him before taking Him into consideration.[44] Unbelief is therefore a corollary of a preconception. It is an applied preconception, not the conclusion of a rational inquiry.

6 THE CHRISTIAN EVENT HAS THE FORM OF AN "ENCOUNTER"

To be recognized, God entered man's life as a man, with a human form, so that man's thought, imagination, and affectivity were, in a way, "blocked," magnetized by Him. The Christian event has the form of an encounter, a human encounter in ordinary day-to-day reality.[45] It has the form of a human encounter in which the man called Jesus, that man born in Bethlehem at a precise moment in time, reveals Himself to be meaningful for our lives. In the Christian event, Jesus's face has the shape of human faces, of companions, of the men He chose, just as, in the villages of Palestine He could not reach, Jesus took on the face of the two disciples He sent there.[46] He arrived in those villages "under" the faces of those two He had chosen. And it was the same thing: "Master, we were able to do the same things as you do."[47] It was identical: "The time has come, the Kingdom of God is at hand."[48]

The Christian event has the form of an encounter: it is something that penetrates our eyes and touches our hearts, something we can take into our arms. For John and Andrew, for each of us, and for everyone who hears about it, it is an encounter. It is an encounter, like when a man is walking along the road holding his child by the hand, and comes across his friend on the opposite sidewalk, and shouts, "Hi! How are you doing? How's your wife?" and then tells the child, "Say good evening," and the child says, "Good evening!" The Christian event is an encounter not a whit less concrete than this. The Christian event has the form of an encounter with a physical, bodily reality, one made of time and space, in which God-made-man is present, and which is a sign of Him. It is an encounter with a present, living, wholly human reality, whose exhaustive meaning is that of being a visible sign of Christ's presence, God-made-man. Encounter therefore means coming across a sacred reality; it is the appearing of the event of the Mystery present within the precariousness of a human form. This encounter is what continually orients our life, imparting meaning and synthesis to our existence. Without it, there is no source of awareness of life's newness. In it, the event of the Mystery that is present touches our lives and makes them part of a continual current of newness.

The impact with an irreducible diversity

What marks the phenomenon of an encounter is a qualitative, perceptible difference in life. To encounter means to come across something different that attracts us because it corresponds to our heart. So it is subjected to the comparison and the judgment of reason, and causes freedom to come forth in affection.

The encounter establishes the impact with something different; it coincides with the experience of a difference that strikes us. But it is different from what? Different from the prevailing mentality, from the usual way of conceiving of what we desire, from the "normal" way of forming a relationship with reality in all its details. What strikes and moves us are people, faces with an identity that appears truer, that corresponds more to our heart, that is less determined by the whole web of factors that make up the social climate as it is favoured by those in power and passively accepted by everyone.

The person we come across becomes an encounter if we find him engaged in a "different" way – with a difference that attracts us – in the things everyone does; if, that is, as he speaks, eats, and drinks, he perceptibly makes a qualitative difference and offers it to our existence, causing us to go away struck by the fact that eating and drinking have an absolute meaning, and a word spoken in fun has an eternal value.[49] Think of those who saw Christ and heard Him speaking, how they must have been struck! Think of John and Andrew before that Man who spoke, as they stood there, watching Him (they did not understand the depth of His thoughts, they did not understand all His words): they had never had such an encounter, they would have never imagined a look, an embrace, and an attention so human, so completely and wholly human, that carried within them something strange, wholly gratuitous, exceptional, beyond everything they could have foreseen. He was so exceptional that it was easy to recognize Him as a divine presence that corresponded to their hearts. Someone who came across Him would never go away again – and this is precisely the sign of an experience of correspondence. An encounter means coming across such an exceptional presence.

An encounter is an all-embracing historical fact

The word "encounter" carries within it the category of historicity; it is precisely this category that sustains and gives consistency to the word encounter. An encounter is a historical fact, it happens at a precise instant in life; it is always tied to a particular moment of our existence. An encounter marks the beginning of a journey, it is a moment made up of time and space. It happens at a precise time, one that you can check on your watch. Life is given to us in order to understand that instant more deeply.

Let's go back to Simon, as he approached Christ, curious to see who He was. When he arrived, Jesus looked at him and said, "You are Simon, son of John, you'll be called Rock."[50] Christ's look penetrates him to the point of understanding his character. Let's imagine what took place in that rough, hearty man. The figure of Christ, whose eyes he had felt understanding him in the depth of his being, immediately established itself as the total horizon of life. Imagine when he went home to his wife and children: he was somewhat "distracted," fully concentrated on the encounter that had just happened, because that encounter defined everything, even though he was not yet aware of it. This

did not make him "slip away" from the relationship with his
wife and children (though probably there were moments when
he appeared distracted by what had happened to him); but that
encounter made him different, truer, with his wife and children.

The encounter that marked the start of our journey has the
same characteristics. It is definitive and all-embracing; all the details of our life story are part of it. The content of the faith – God
made man, Jesus Christ who died and is risen – that emerges in
an encounter, at a point in history, embraces all its moments and
aspects, which are brought as if by a whirlpool into that encounter, and must be faced from its standpoint, according to the love
that springs from it, according to the possibility of its usefulness
for one's own destiny and for the destiny of man it points to. The
encounter we have had, which is all-encompassing by its very
nature, in time becomes the true shape of every relationship, the
true form by which I look at nature, at myself, at others, and
at things. When an encounter is all-embracing, it becomes the
shape, not only the sphere, of relationships. It not only establishes a companionship as the place where relationships exist but
it is the form by which they are conceived of and lived out.

7 FAITH IS PART OF THE CHRISTIAN EVENT

The attitude of one who is struck by the Christian event, who
recognizes it and adheres to it, is called "faith."[51]

Our position regarding the event of Christ is the same as that
of Zacchaeus before that Man who stopped under the tree that
he had climbed, and told him, "Come down, quickly, I am coming to your place."[52] It is the same position as that of the widow
whose only son had died, and who heard Jesus saying, in a way
that appears so irrational to us, "Woman, do not weep!"[53] It
is absurd to say such a thing to a mother whose only son has
died. For them, as for us, it was the experience of the presence of
something radically different from what we imagine, and at the
same time something that totally and originally corresponds to
the profound expectations of our person. To experience a total

correspondence with our heart is something absolutely exceptional. In fact, the word "exceptional" exactly denotes the experience of such a correspondence. Since our heart is made for this correspondence, it should be something normal in life, but, on the contrary, it never happens. When it does happen, it is an exceptional experience. Faith is having the sincerity to recognize, the simplicity to accept, and the affection to cling to such a Presence.

Sincerity and simplicity are analogous words. To be simple means to look something in the face, without bringing in extraneous factors borrowed from outside. The fact that Christianity is an event is hard for most people to accept, because something foreign to such an announcement slips in: a trendy opinion, the preconception that determines the current mentality, the nihilism that prevails, facile skepticism. Rather we must look at the fact, at the event, with simplicity; in other words, we must look at the event for what it says, for what it communicates to reason, what it communicates to the heart, without bringing in external factors to evaluate it, for they have nothing to do with it. Analogously, one looks "sincerely" at a message if one looks at how it is brought, and at what it says, without introducing ifs, buts, and maybes, the rapid-fire ways by which the imposture that lurks in man – the lack of a real desire for the truth – separates us from reality, disturbs our contact with it, makes us run away, preventing us from knowing it and judging it. The opposite of sincerity, that is, what is bogus, false, points to the introduction of something foreign into the relationship with reality.

Being simple and sincere means to exclude the ifs, buts and maybes, and to speak plainly. "He gave sight to a man born blind," says St John's gospel: all that the Pharisees said and objected to had nothing to do with what had happened. It was born out of something foreign to the fact, from a preconception that was already in them. On the contrary, the man born blind said, "I could not see before, now I can see. Therefore this man is a prophet, because God does not do things like this for no reason."[54] The blind man looked at the event that had touched him with simplicity and sincerity. In considering an object, especially if it has to do with life, we go wrong when we allow questions and factors foreign to the object to creep in. They alter our relationship with it and hamper our affection for it.

To know, we need an attitude of openness, that is, of "love."[55] Without love man cannot know. After all, this love is manifest in that original instinct with which nature – in other words, God who creates us – launches us, through our curiosity, into a universal comparison. Man naturally reaches out to reality with curiosity, and this is the affirmation of an ineffable positivity. Replacing the original attitude – curiosity – with ifs, buts and maybes, approaching reality with our arm shielding our eyes, is a lack of sincerity and simplicity. In the end, only that lively openness to the object that becomes affection enables the object to touch us for what it is (*affici,* to be touched by). Just as man walks with his whole self, he sees with his whole self, too. He sees with the eyes of reason insofar as his heart is open, that is to say, insofar as affection keeps his eyes open; otherwise his eyes close before the object, they "go to sleep," they turn away. Thus, the eye of reason sees to the degree that it is sustained by affection, which already expresses freedom's engagement.

A person recognizes Christ's presence because Christ wins the person over. In other words, faith can only happen in man and in the world if something that is grace, pure grace happens first: the Christ event, the encounter with Christ, in which man experiences something exceptional that cannot happen on its own.[56]

Essentially, faith is recognizing a Presence that is different, recognizing an exceptional, divine presence. What is exceptional does not normally happen, and when it happens one says, "This is something quite different. There is a super-human power here!" Think of how many times the Samaritan woman had thirsted for the attitude with which Christ treated her in that instant. She had never realized it before, but when it happened she recognized it.[57]

Faith is part of the Christian event because it is part of the grace that the event represents, part of what it is. Faith belongs to the event because, as *loving recognition* of the presence of something exceptional, it is a gift, it is a grace.[58] Just as Christ gives

Himself to me in a present event, He brings to life within me the capacity for grasping it and recognizing it in its exceptionality. Thus my freedom accepts that event, and acknowledges it. So in us, faith is both the recognition of the exceptional that is present and the simple and sincere adherence that says "Yes" and does not object. Recognition and adherence are part of the moment in which the Lord reveals Himself to us through the power of His Spirit. They are part of the moment when the event of Christ enters our life. To recognize Him in life is a gift of the Spirit, which always implies a simplicity of heart, the assertion of an original candour that is part of our origin. For God creates us with our eyes and heart wide open to reality, positively reaching out to it, so that when we meet something we can say, "This is it." God creates man with this positive outlook and this affection for reality.[59]

Recognizing Christ is a grace, and it is a gift of ourselves to Him in original simplicity. The event of Christ is God's love for man recognized by man's love for God. Only hatred for Being can ultimately refuse the opportunity to recognize Him. And hatred for Being is the opposite of what we are originally, the opposite of how man is conceived in his mother's womb. This is why in St Matthew's Gospel Jesus says, "I thank You Father because you have hidden these things from the wise and have revealed them to the humble."[60]

The loving acknowledgment of an exceptional presence

Faith is the "acknowledgment" that God has become a factor of present experience. As acknowledgment, it is an act of reason, a judgment, rather than a feeling or a state of mind. Faith is the fulfillment of human reason. It is the intelligence of reality in its ultimate horizon, the recognition of That in which everything consists.[61] Natural intelligence cannot reach this ultimate horizon. It is only through something that has happened, through the event of God-made-man, through His gift, that our renewed intelligence can recognize and touch Him. Thus faith reaches an apex beyond reason: without faith, reason is not complete, whereas, in faith, reason becomes the ladder of hope. Faith is rational, for it flourishes on the extreme boundary of the rational dynamic as a flower of grace to which man adheres with his freedom. How can man adhere to this flower with his freedom, this flower that is incomprehensible in both its origin and in its making? For man, adhering with his freedom means unhesitatingly recognizing with simplicity what his reason perceives as exceptional, as he does with the unassailable, indestructible evidence of factors and moments in reality as they enter his own personal horizon.[62]

Since it is a knowledge that lets itself be totally determined by the object, faith is a "loving" recognition. It is a loving knowledge, one that is simple and unequivocal, one that implies an attachment. This loving knowledge makes us say, as it made Peter say, "If I were not to believe this man I could not even believe my own eyes."[63]

Since the object of faith is the normal and proper object of reason – its object is the divine that is present (not the divine, but the "divine-present" in the human) – for us to recognize it, it is necessary first of all that it manifest itself through an exceptional presence. This exceptionality "captures" man's heart (think of the Samaritan woman),[64] so that we can recognize it and adhere to it in virtue of a correspondence we have perceived. This perception leads us to welcome it without delay and to adhere to it wholeheartedly; the entire self, intelligence and affection, is moved in this acknowledgment laden with love. Thus man can say, "All that You have done, all that You have said corresponds so deeply to me that I cannot help recognizing present in You that which You are."

Man's contribution, then, lies in the fact that man is able to cry out, "Christ, save me!" Man's freedom is summed up in the entreaty, "Accepting that all is grace, I ask you for grace." This is how we completely take into account both the fact that all is grace and the fact that, for its effect, Christ's grace depends on my freedom, too. Everything starts off from the acknowledgment of a gift already given.[65] Entreaty is the point of marriage, the point of spousal union, between man's freedom and Christ: "The

Spirit and the Bride say, Come!"[66] Man's part is entreaty, the cry of the beggar, the cry of expectation, or the delight of desire.

Entreaty and offering

So the question arises when faced with a Presence, otherwise it is not a reasonable question. Now you don't have to have completed the journey to acknowledge the Presence. The question launches the journey, an itinerary of questions addressed to a You who is present. "Who are You?" as the astonished Twelve[67] asked Him, and as Pascoli's confused blind man[68] asks. Without this itinerary of questions, the initial question was not a true one either.

The initial correspondence between the present divine and the expectation of the heart sets the premise for a journey in which the Other, Christ, in the end answers "I am God."[69] One who has experienced the wonder of correspondence will kneel down and adore Him. He will say yes to Him. This is the journey Zacchaeus made.[70] After Simon, he is the most significant figure from this point of view. Nothing is more human than what Zacchaeus felt when he felt that Man looking at him, that Man who said to him, "Come down, I am coming to your place." He must not even have thought of God in that moment. But later he must have pondered, or at least thought back to, what that Man had said to him. Outstripping his every imagination, Jesus had disconcerted him so much that, from that moment on, he lived totally defined by that encounter. The same happened to Peter: when faced with Jesus's question ("Who do you say I am?") he answered impetuously, "You are the Christ, the Son of the Living God."[71]

Man's answer to Christ's request is the entreaty to be able to respond to His request, for nothing can happen except through grace. If this starting point is made clear, we still have the pretension of being able to answer by ourselves and of being able to adhere by ourselves. Peter's answer does not make him immediately able to love Christ; that is to say, it does not make him automatically consistent. Peter wants to love Christ. In him there is the recognition of Christ, and as a consequence he should adhere to Christ, and do what Christ tells him to do. Yet he is a sinner

("Get behind me").[72] Even when faced with the question, "Do you love me?" he must have felt really ashamed! He answered, "Lord, You know I love you."[73] This statement is tantamount to recognizing that the ultimate horizon of one's life and of everything is His Presence, and asking to adhere to It.

Offering is the ultimate consequence of faith.[74] It is just saying, "O Lord, You know I love You." Offering does not require a tremendous effort, but only "I recognize who You are." And one cannot say, "I recognize who You are" without feeling that one is plunging into the humiliation of one's sinful nothingness, and, paradoxically, without at the same time perceiving the beginning of freedom, which becomes an entreaty to the One who is present and has created the request.

8 A FACT IN THE PRESENT, A FACT IN THE PAST

John and Andrew went home that night and said, "We have found the Messiah."[75] They had had an encounter – it was an event that was happening in the present – one that claimed to hold the exhaustive meaning of their lives. But where was the root of what that encounter meant, where was the content of that encounter? In an unforeseeable way, that event fulfilled a history of the past. In that history, the proclamation of the claim had begun, and within its context it was possible to explain the content of the encounter that was taking place. It was the great history of the Jewish people (the Law, the Prophets, the Psalms), begun with Abraham and arising out of God's promise that he would be the starting point of a great people who would carry the meaning of the whole world – as Isaiah says, speaking not only of Israel, but of all nations.[76]

John and Andrew – and the same applies to the two disciples of Emmaus – had Jesus before their eyes,[77] but the claim of total meaning for their lives carried by that event referred to a past in which that event had been the object of prophecy; from the present a memory welled up whose content began in the past. They could not explain Christ without beginning to consider what they had never consciously taken into account in their lives, i.e., the fact that God had promised His coming to expectant man: "*Rorate, coeli desuper, et nubes pluant Justum.*"[78] It was an encounter that fulfilled a previous beginning.

Memory

It is the same for us now. The encounter that happens today is a source of memory because it means coming across a presence that begins in the past. Polycarp, bishop of Smyrna, was deeply moved whenever he told of his teacher John (who was already old when they first met), and of how he would talk of that afternoon when, with Andrew, he had set eyes on Jesus for the first time. (Polycarp would later give up his life for Christ, burned at the stake).[79] He had his encounter with Christ through John. For him, the encounter with Christ had the face, the characteristics, the form of John, of the Christians of Smyrna and the leader of that community. Yet that encounter that gave rise to Polycarp's faith drew all its value, its content, its consistency from Jesus of Nazareth, born of Mary: the Man who, that afternoon, after receiving baptism from John the Baptist, had gone home followed by those two who did not dare speak to Him. This is why an encounter is the source of memory. What struck Polycarp in that moment was a fact in the present: "Jesus is the same yesterday, today and forever!"[80] but it was a fact that had begun years before.

"Memory" indicates the historical depth of an encounter, as far back as the root from which it ultimately started. The encounter we have today is true because He, Jesus Christ, born of the Virgin Mary, died and rose, ascended into heaven and affects reality with His Spirit. This encounter finds its value in a Fact that took place 2,000 years ago. Faith is the awareness of a presence that began in the past. This is why an encounter activates memory.[81]

Let us dwell again on the word "encounter." It does not indicate merely coming across something that moves into the horizon of our existence, but the happening within this horizon of a presence capable of changing life altogether. Thus an encounter earns the right to be called an "event" in the full sense of the term. An encounter is characterized as the impact with something exceptional, capable of "metamorphosing" life, changing its shape, its outline, so as to create a new world.[82]

In an encounter, faith begins because it carries, bears, makes present something exceptional, unforeseen, unforeseeable, which radically strikes our life, so as to change its principle of cognition, its principle of affection and its capacity to build, calling it to collaborate creatively with God's plan, which would otherwise be ineffable. The word "memory" is crucially enlightening precisely because it indicates that the encounter we have today finds its root in a past. The present encounter makes us discover the original event, which in turn is the foundation of, and is decisive for the truth of, the present encounter. It explains it. The word memory, therefore, describes the history between the event at its origin and the encounter that makes the original event an unavoidable, indestructible, undeniable presence. The whole wealth of the beginning is within the present and it is in the present that man discovers the divinity of the origin. Memory is the history that runs from the origin up to the present. The material content (thought, affection, work) of the word memory is also called Tradition.

From the past and from the present

So it is possible to describe the dynamic of the Christian event both by starting from the past and moving towards the present and by starting from the present and moving towards the past. We can sum it up in the following formulations: *a) an event in the past* that claims a meaning for one's life *can be found in the experience of a present event,* which is the beginning of a memory whose content is fully explained within the past event; *b) a present event,* one that claims to have a definitive and all-embracing meaning for one's life, *can be explained only in virtue of an event in the past* in which this claim began and which we reach through a memory of the content of that time that is fulfilled now. It is in a present event that man today discovers an event in the past that has the same claim to meaning; just as the present event establishes a memory that has its ultimate content in that past event.

Apologetic value and educative value

These formulations are valuable from both the apologetic and pedagogical points of view. The apologetic, demonstrative path unfolds in the first way; the educative path in the second. The first formulation is important for countering any clerical attempt to stand before the the the world, to impose ourselves on the world, or to justify ourselves in the world's eyes with a hegemonic and ideological claim. In recent decades, for instance, people have all too often tried to justify Christianity's validity in terms of the dominant values of the culture of the moment. This led to the obliteration of the essential fact that, after 2,000 years, Christianity is an *original* presence today, one that carries the claim of a meaning for the life that began then. And the fully adequate understanding of the fact in the past is enlightened in the encounter with a *present* event that is laden with promise for life. The world's well-being is a consequence of this present event, which is brought to fulfillment according to the will of God, according to the measure of His gifts.

Instead, the second formulation, above all, has an educational, clarifying value: it makes us understand that what we experience today in Christian life is what the medieval monks lived, and is what John and Andrew lived even before them. All the educative work that needs to be carried out, especially with youth, depends on this, so that, by starting from the fascination of the encounter, they may come to realize all that it implies.

We realize what has happened, starting 2,000 years ago, because we are struck by and we adhere to a proposal that comes to us in the present, before which it is possible to say, "The meaning of life is right here." Thus we discover all that is implied in the fact we encounter, and the content of memory begins to unfold. Laurence the Hermit says, "I was told, All must be taken in without words and safeguarded in silence; then I understood that perhaps the whole of my life would be spent in recalling what had happened to me. And the memory of You fills me with silence."

2

The Event Goes on in History (the Temple in Time)

1 THE EVENT GOES ON IN HISTORY THROUGH THE COMPANIONSHIP OF THE BELIEVERS

The Event of Christ goes on in history through the companionship of the believers, which is a sign, like a tent in which dwells the Holy of Holies, the Mystery made man. This Mystery goes on in the life of every man and the life of the world, personally and in reality, through the tangibly expressed unity of Christians. The companionship of the believers is the effective sign of Christ's salvation for men;[1] it is the sacrament of the world's salvation.

This is how the risen Christ holds us in His embrace; this companionship is Christ Himself present. It is Christ in His human reality. It is the body of Christ that becomes present, so that we touch Him, we see Him, we feel Him. The value of this companionship is deeper than appearances, because what we see is the emergence of the Mystery of Christ revealing itself.

The word "body" does not encompass all a person is. It describes what appears and what can be seen of what a person is. All the same, this "appearance," this visibility, is real. The body is something real, visible, and tangible. The believers are part of this visible Body, which is much deeper than what is seen. It has a value that exceeds the human reality of its components. It has a root that penetrates into a land unknown to us, the land of Being, the land of Mystery.

To introduce ourselves to the understanding of the Mystery of Christ's Body we can, by analogy, think of the mystery of the human personality, which communicates itself through the body. The body does not reveal the whole of one's personality, but is the continuous beginning of the endless, mysterious journey into it. What is seen, heard, and touched, what can be experienced of the other and his behaviour, continuously reveals something of what the other is, something of the mystery of his self. By analogy, the companionship through which Christ embraces us makes us know better who Christ is. It reveals to us what He is for us.

Jesus Christ is present here and now. He goes on being present in history through the uninterrupted succession of men who belong to Him through the action of His Spirit, as members of His Body, the prolongation of His Presence in time and space.[2] Baptism is the action with which Christ, died and risen, grasps those who the Father has put into his hands and takes them up into Himself.[3] In this way they become part of His figure, of His personality, members of His Body. So Christ is like a body that grows in time, a personality that becomes more and more evident in history; as St Paul says, "Until we all attain to the unity of faith and knowledge of the Son of God, to mature manhood, to the measure of the stature of the fullness of Christ."[4]

"Saul, Saul, why are you persecuting me?"

Let's go to the page of the New Testament in which this factor, the community of the believers, emerges in history. Here we literally witness the birth of a new, irresistible protagonist. Saul was on his way to Damascus, in command of a platoon of soldiers, to arrest the Christians of that city and put them in prison. At a certain point of the journey, a light envelops him and throws him to the ground. As he falls he hears a powerful voice, "Saul, Saul, why are you persecuting *me*?"[5] Here, in the question addressed to Saul, a company of men suddenly emerges as a new factor in history. Saul was persecuting people who, for the most part, he had never met (maybe some of them had seen him). "Saul, Saul, why are you persecuting *me*?" This establishes an identity between people who were strangers to him, and who he was on his way to persecute, and that Being whose voice in that moment filled earth and heaven, in other words his whole life, overwhelming it forever, making him the starting point of a triumphant battle destined to fill all of time and history.

Let's try to imagine ourselves in the place of one of the members of the early Christian community in Damascus. The question addressed to Saul establishes an identity between me, living in Damascus, scraping together a living making carpets, and that Man I heard old Ananias talking about, a man called Jesus of Nazareth, son of Mary. As we have recalled, that day in Nain, on seeing a widowed mother following the bier of her dead son, this Jesus was gripped by the impulse of emotion and, stepping forward, put a hand on her shoulder and said to her, "Woman, don't cry," a strange thing to say. Then he raised her son to life.[6] But how can you say such a thing to a widow who has just lost her son? It's absurd. And yet it was this very "absurdity" that left the people agape. And I, too, stood there agape and said, "Yes, there is the source of life; that Man is the source of life." He had said, "I am the Resurrection and the Life."[7] Yes, that Man is the Way, the Resurrection and the Life.[8] So I joined the Damascus group and am now about to be persecuted, put in jail, and maybe put to death by Saul. Though he doesn't know me, he is coming to persecute me because I am identified with that Man who met John and Andrew,[9] that Man who raised that widow's son to life, who told Zacchaeus, "Come down, because I am coming to eat at your house,"[10] who took a child in his arms, held it to his breast and said, "Woe to whomever puts a stumbling block before the smallest of these children."[11] I am one with that Man, with that Man who one day, after climbing a hill, turned to look at the crowd following him, and felt pity for them because they were like sheep without a shepherd,[12] a symbol, as it were, of the whole of mankind. I am one with Him, and whoever persecutes me persecutes Him. "Saul, Saul, why are you persecuting *me*?" That "persecuting *me*" indicates that He and I are one, identified together: we have become one. That "*me*" reveals that Christians and Christ Himself are the same thing.

Some years later, St Paul wrote down what he had understood from that moment: that Christians and Christ are one. Those who have been taken hold of by the action of baptism have entered Christ and have become one with Him. "You who have been baptized in Christ have become one with Christ."[13] So there is no longer any difference. "There is no longer Jew nor Greek (the great cultural difference at the time), no slave nor freeman (the great social divide), no man nor woman, since you are all one in Christ Jesus."[14] You are all one, *eis*,[15] a single being, one in Christ Jesus. This is the unity that that man who had fallen down on the Damascus Road discovered, confusedly, when he heard himself asked, "Saul, Saul, why are you persecuting *me?*"

Unity with Christ means the unity amongst Christians. Thus, a short time later, St Paul was able to observe, "we who share in the one bread" are one.[16] We are one in the ontological sense of the word, so much so that each of us is a member of the same body. In fact, to point out the wrong way people were treating each other in the Ephesus community, St Paul wrote, "Don't you know you are members of each other?"[17] Not only members of Christ, therefore, but members of each other. The relationship between Christ and me, between Christ and you, is the relationship between you and me. There is no wrong that can become an objection or offer resistance to this unity.

The greatest revolution is a humanly tangible unity

Whoever believes in Christ and tries to follow Him, though he remains a mere man, shares in that one reality that is capable of changing the world, the reality that man most desires and yet finds most impossible: unity amongst men.

The need for unity lies at the root of the whole expression of man's life, it belongs to the definition of his "I." Every great human revolution has had universalism as its supreme ideal – to make the whole of humanity one. The supreme ideal of every philosophy, too, has been the unity of mankind, a unity in which each one can be himself and yet be one with others. But no philosophy has ever been able to imagine it in a precise way and no revolution has managed to bring it about. In the end despair destroys the revolutionary ideal because it turns out to be impossible to achieve.

The more man tries to realize his original aspiration to unity, the more this unity reveals itself to be impossible, beyond the reach of his powers. Not even the unity between man and woman, between parents and children, appears possible; one is tempted to say that this, above all, is impossible. How can we come to love others? How can we come to have compassion for others? How can we come to an experience of unity in which our need for companionship is satisfied?

This need for companionship is unavoidable since it belongs to the essence of the self. So there is nothing more deceptive than the will to stay on one's own or to be alone. For in solitude man is badly off, he refuses himself. Only if the presence of another is a dimension of life, then, even though it may not be more fulfilled, at least one lives life, one accepts it. Companionship belongs to the essence of what is, to the Mystery of which all things are made – the Mystery of Being is Trinity, it is the absolute One and at the same time Communion. Man's original need for unity can be understood only in the light of God as one and three. Ultimate Being is communion in its own mysterious substance. It is certainly mysterious – we would not be able to understand. It was revealed to us when the Mystery made Himself known to us in this way: "The Father and I are one."[18]

Not only has it been made known to us, we are made to share in it. For how can one say "you," and therefore say "I"? How is it possible to become one with others? Through the grace of an Event. Man can say "you," he can be one with another because Someone has come into the world who said, "I am the Way, the Truth and the Life,"[19] the expression of the goodwill of the Mystery who makes all things, and who has become man's companion on his journey full of trials. It is this Man who makes my life capable of companionship and, in this companionship, allows it to activate its capacity for bearing fruit, its creativity. How? By grasping me and drawing me into Himself, by assimilating me into His personality and making me become a member of His body, through the action of His Spirit, the energy with which He penetrates time and space,[20] and grasps the man the Father places in His hands. The Spirit of Christ, who reaches me through the concrete circumstances of time and space, makes me discover what my self is and what others are – each one made for the Other because every man belongs to Him; so I and the others are one, members of each other.

To live the mystery of the Church, in other words, the unity between those chosen by Christ, constitutes the greatest miracle, which reveals to the confusion of human spirits the presence of the Mystery that makes all things.

"Christ is everything in everyone."[21] Unity is the supreme category of being and of truth, as deeply desired as it is inconceivable. St Gregory of Nyssa writes, "Amongst all the all-embracing words that Christ addresses to the Father there is one greater than all others and that summarizes all others. It is that in which Christ warns his own to be always united in solving questions and in the valuation of the good to be done."[22] The phenomenon that best demonstrates God's power is precisely the unity of those who acknowledge Him. The new way of looking at others and of dealing with each other testifies to His Presence in the most convincing way for human reason. In the new way in which I look at others, and in the way I say "you," all sense of foreignness is abolished, everything tends towards unity.

Christ is present *here and now* for us in the unity we are called to live, in the Church. The greatest thing that can be seen in the world is for people to be united as members of one Body, not because they are committed to a particular task, but because they are called by the same act of Christ, by one identical event, so that, although they were totally unknown to each other, complete strangers up to that moment, they are, and acknowledge themselves to be, bound to one another in a way beyond compare. St Paul joins those who he had first been persecuting, "he went to Jerusalem and came back with them, speaking openly in the Lord's name," arousing astonishment and even rage in those who saw persecuted and persecutor together.[23]

The revolutionary ideal of unity came true with Christ, beginning with two men, called John and Andrew. After a few days there were five or six of them, then there were twelve. Later, others came along and they grew into a group who would meet under Solomon's portico.[24] As time went by, there were more and more of them; they invaded Europe and changed its human makeup. From that Man, through the Spirit of that Man died and risen, who dominates time and space, so powerful as to defeat death, this unity has reached us – so that through our unity He might become salvation for the world today.

The "companionship" we are speaking of is thus not a reality that we have made or discovered. This companionship is willed, given consistency, and made permanent by an Other. "The Spirit that hovered over the water"[25] made a cosmos, an ordered world, out of chaos, just as the same Spirit makes a cosmos, an order[26] out of the chaos of people who were strangers to each other, far from each other. The precise term that reveals the ontology, the ultimate nature of this human cosmos is "communion." This is what makes us members of Christ and members of each other, belonging to one Body, Christ's Body.[27] Christ does not exist in history without us, but there is no "us," no communion among us, without Christ. If we try to discern this word at the moment of its birth in a mysterious and fascinating glimpse, this "companionship" – as the condition for man's existence in reality and in history – emerges where man is chosen, where the Fact, the Event of election, sets to work in history.

2 THE GENERATIVE AND DYNAMIC LAW OF "COMPANIONSHIP": ELECTION

The spread of Christ's Body, the Church, the spread of this mysterious unity, is the peak and the meaning of creation that Christ's Spirit carries out, bearing down on worldly reality, time, and space like a wind, continually transforming it. The event of this organism that God awakened to be the rallying point and the horizon in the world, the point of departure and the final aim of everything, has a law of generation, which is also the law of its development. The kingdom of Christ is like a great organism whose law of creation and growth to the point of fulfilling its destiny, its final end, which is the full glory of Christ,[28] is the law of choice or election. In order that Christ be "everything in everyone,"[29] in order that the glory of Christ appear as the form and content of all things ("In him all things hold together"),[30] God, the Mystery, the Father's Word, makes a choice or election, a call.

The great teacher

The history of the Hebrew people is the foretelling of what was to happen to the whole of mankind.[31] If we read the history of the Hebrew people with intelligence and humility, and with affection for the Mystery of Being, for the Mystery of the Father, we can easily recognize these lines of development, these hints at the aim.

"It was not because you were more in number than any other people that the LORD set his love upon you and chose you, for you were the fewest of all peoples; but it is because the LORD loves you, and is keeping the oath which he swore to your fathers, that the LORD has brought you out with a mighty hand, and redeemed you from the house of bondage, from the hand of the Pharaoh king of Egypt. Know therefore that the LORD your God is God, the faithful God who keeps covenant and steadfast love with those who love him and keep his commandments, to a thousand generations."[32]

St Paul considers the history of the Hebrew people "the great teacher,"[33] the great teacher whom God has created, formulated, assisted, destined, to prepare the whole of mankind for salvation. The preparation that the Hebrew people is for the great event of His Revelation in human nature, the education that it represents, is of more value to us who come later than for the people of that time, who did not know and did not recognize the meaning of the Hebrew people. Throughout its history, this people was made by God as an education, as an introduction that would shed light on the nature of His intervention in the world, in history. For the people of that time it was like a light in the darkness; for us it is like realizing that it will be a fine day, when the light has already dawned and the sun has already begun its course, opening up a path even within the space of our distraction.

Christ the one Sent

The great call, the great choice, the great election that God has made in His plan for the world is the call of Christ, the Man who said, "What I see the Father doing, I do always. I do nothing but what I see my Father doing."[34] This mysterious and eternal election of Christ is the great call that embraces everything and explains everything: the world, the life of each and everyone, the history of peoples and their migrations, whose aim, according to St Paul, is the search for God, for the plan God has for their existence and movement.[35] The election of Jesus Christ coincides with the mission of making the mysterious plan of the Father for all things visible. "I was sent for this."[36] If anyone living at the time of Christ were to have asked Him, "Who are you? What is your name?" Jesus could have replied, "I am the one sent by the Father" (missus, the one sent by the Father).[37] "Sent by an Other": this expression implies the mystery regarding His origin and His end, the total mystery of his person, which, since it could be experienced and met and touched existentially, is related to the meaning of this word "sent." If we read chapters five to eight of John's Gospel, and then the final chapters, thirteen to seventeen, the word that Christ uses most often in referring to himself is "sent." John speaks insistently of Christ's reply: I am "the one sent by the Father,"[38] the expression amongst men of the Mystery of the Father, the presence amongst men of the Mystery who makes all things, to whom all men are subject.

In His most dramatic dialogues, Jesus often used this definition of Himself as the content of His answers. "My Father goes on working and so do I," "the Son can do nothing of himself except what he sees the Father doing; what He does the Son does, too," "I can do nothing by myself," "the works that the Father gave me to do witness that the Father sent me. And the Father who sent me bears witness to me."[39] And again in chapters six, seven, and eight, "I came down from heaven not to do my own will, but the will of Him who sent me. And this is the will of the one who sent me, that I should lose nothing of what He has given me"; "no one comes to me unless he is drawn by the Father who sent me."[40] "My teaching is not my own, but of the One who sent me." I did not come of my own will, and the one who sent me is truthful and you do not know Him."[41] "See, I am not alone, I and the Father who sent me are one." "The one who sent me is truthful, and I tell the world what I have heard from Him"; "I do nothing of myself, but as the Father has told me, so I speak. The one who sent me is with me, He does not leave me alone."[42]

The same awareness of being the one sent by the Father is expressed, as we mentioned, in chapters 13-17. "Jesus, knowing that the Father had put everything in his hands and that He had come from God and was going back to God."[43] Thus begins chapter thirteen of John's Gospel, which introduces the account of the Passion. "If you know me, you will know the Father, too." "Whoever has seen me has seen the Father." "I am in the Father and you are in me." "The world needs to know that I love the Father and do what the Father has commanded me."[44] "Everything I have heard from the Father I have made known to you"; "they have seen my works and have hated me and my Father."[45] "All that the Father has is mine"; "I came from the Father and have come into the world"; "You will all scatter, but I am not alone because the Father is with me."[46] "Father, the hour has come, glorify your son so that the Son may glorify you. You have given Him power over every human being"; "I have made your name known to men, to those you have given me in the world"; "All that you have given me comes from you"; "All that is mine is yours and all that is yours is mine"; "As you Father have sent me, so I am sending them into the world"; "Righteous Father, the World has not known you, but I have known you and these know that you have sent me because I made your name known to them and will make it known, so that the love with which you loved me may be in them and I in them."[47] The discovery of all the expressions in John's Gospel in which Jesus

asserts His awareness of being sent by the Father stirs up great
emotion regarding the Mystery, because in the Person of Christ
this Mystery reveals itself as the meaning of human history and
of reality as a whole.

Let's see now how, in that history that bears the name of the
month and the year of our birth, in the history of men and
of the world, this election of Jesus, which is His mission, is expressed as *elegkhos*, the Greek word meaning to prove oneself,
reaching down to us.

The choice of Mary[48]

Our Lady, this young woman, fifteen or seventeen years old, was
chosen to be and to create the first dwelling place, the first temple
of God in the world,[49] the temple of the true, living God. Mary
was chosen to be God's first home in the world, the first context,
the first milieu, the first place in which everything belonged to
God, who was coming to live amongst us. All that she is – all – is
for God, His dwelling. *Gratia plena*. So she is beautiful (*Virgo
pulcherrima*), since beauty is the splendour of the truth.

And the "house" of Nazareth – of all the rest, this is what is
most striking in a pilgrimage to the Holy Land. How stirring
when, from just above it, you read on the stone below: "Verbum
caro hic factum est," "The Word was made flesh *here*," here! –
It is the first development of that house that is Mary's womb,
that is Mary. This is the earliest development of that personality
totally taken hold of by God, which was totally "for" Christ,
made, existing, alive, living, creative, full of grace, so that Christ
be acknowledged. This house was the first development of the
first human dwelling of the Mystery, which is Our Lady.

The body of Christ which spreads
in time and space: the Church

The reality of the house of Nazareth is a place made of time
and space in which everything is for Christ. This reality, this human dwelling of the Mystery, spread throughout the world. We

can say it. St Paul could say "It is spreading."[50] We instead say, "It has spread" throughout the world. In this spreading, who is the mediator, who makes everything in its sphere all for Christ? Man, the man who is called, the man who is chosen, the one who answers, the man sent to fulfill a mission entrusted to him by Christ ("as the Father sent me, so I am sending you"): this man renews the world, he is the visible protagonist of its redemption.

The reality of the house of Nazareth has spread throughout the world through the choice of men constituted together as a form, a single reality: the Church, the Body of Christ which spreads in time and space, the presence of Him who was born of Our Lady, in His ongoing birth in the world, the event of Christ present in the world in every moment (years, months, days, hours, and minutes) of history; it is the Church as the mysterious Body of the Risen Christ, which spreads in the world by the action of His Spirit.

For what is the power that allows the on-going development of that organism, the permanence, the renewal, and the multiplication of that dwelling made of the living reality of those who are called? What is the power that allows this spread of the Church? That which allows this on-going development is the Fact itself, the Guest of that house that was Our Lady's womb. This Guest, the King of the universe, "*cunctorum dominator alme*," died on the cross and rose so that everyone should understand that He is the King of the Universe. After a few weeks He ascended to heaven, that is to say He descended into the depths where things are born, where everything is generated, where everything is created, moment by moment, and from there sent His Spirit, the Creator Spirit, into the world: "*Veni Creator Spiritus*." The summit and meaning of His Spirit's creation, the Spirit who, like the wind, imbues the whole of worldly reality, time, and space, continually transforming it, is the spread of the Church. This history carries the meaning of the world, the meaning of the whole of world history.

Christ makes Himself known, makes Himself accessible and therefore gives us His Spirit in the Church by means of Holy Scripture, the Sacraments, and the Apostolic Succession, but above all the Holy Spirit strikes us and invades us through the life of the Church as a whole. The Church is the universe reached, recreated, and possessed by Christ though His Spirit. In other words, the Church is mankind inasmuch as it is made true, made one, by the presence of Christ, by means of that re-creative energy which is the mystery of the Spirit at Pentecost.[51] If He were not present in the living Church, Christ would be irremediably far off and therefore a prey to our interpretation.

Were He not to offer Himself to us in the mystery of His Body, which is the Church, Christ would end up being subjectively reduced, in both content and method. So the Church is the method with which Christ communicates Himself in time and space, analogously to the fact that Christ is the method with which God chose to communicate himself to men for their salvation. Through the Church's humanity, the divine reaches us both as "communication of the truth" (Scripture, Tradition, Magisterium)[52] and therefore as a help to man for reaching an objective clarity and certainty in perceiving the ultimate meaning of his own existence, and as "communication of the divine reality" – Grace – through the Sacraments.[53] In the Church, God makes Himself familiar to man in every age. The familiarity of God's day-to-day relationship with us is also expressed – in a particularly convincing way – in events and persons that refer directly to Him: miracle and holiness.

Miracle is the happening of something that "forces" one to think of God. This can have a personal and "private" effect or a more public and grandiose value. God's relationship with us is totally exceptional. If He is creator, then He is creator in every instant; in every instant He is forming me; in every instant I am being made by Him. But God's way of relating to us tends to express our being made by Him, created by Him, in a familiar way – like a mother tends to express her love for her child many times a day, every day, with a look, a caress, a kiss, an affectionate greeting. So a miracle is an event, something that happens that I did not foresee and that I cannot explain, that "forces" me to think of God. It doesn't necessarily force others, though. The Church draws a distinction between a miracle that has a private value, whose aim is to draw the attention of the one it happens to, or to someone near him – if it happens to a friend of yours, you will inexorably think of God, too – and a miracle that is so enormous that it can be clearly documented and can thus be told to people of all times.[54]

We spoke of miracle and *holiness*. In the reality of the Church of all times there can be seen figures with a human stature that measures up to the truest desires of the human heart: the saints. In these an exceptional humanity is realized, one impossible to imagine, inconceivably pure, coherent, powerful, though still within the same fragility as everyone else's humanity. The humanity of the saints is just like my own, but Something greater[55] blossoms within it, Something that I and every other man need, but are unable to accomplish. But "what is impossible to man is not impossible to God."[56] Jesus Christ is not an isolated presence far back in history, so as to seem a product of the imagination. He is a Presence ten years after His death, a thousand years, two thousand years after His death, right up to the present day, through that new humanity of the saints, an unimaginable human presence.

Men called

The blossoming of an exceptional humanity is part of the dynamics that generates the new companionship that is the Church. Christ calls some so that all may become aware of His event. Now is this not unjust? Why only those whom He calls and not everyone? He calls everyone, as St Paul says,[57] but by means of a method that gets one person after another involved with Him. He called some so that they would communicate Him to others, and these again to others, in a flow of humanity that has come down to me now so as to reach others through me. "God raised Jesus on the third day and wanted Him to appear not to all the people, but to the witnesses He had chosen: to us who ate and drank with Him after His resurrection from the dead. And He has commanded us to proclaim to the people that He is the judge of the living and the dead."[58]

In the passage from *Acts*, the term that stands at the top of the list, the most profound, that on which faith, the encounter, and the

whole architecture of memory stand, is the word "chosen," "pre-
selected" by the Father. This term indicates the foundation of everything, the origin of that flower which sprouts in Our Lady's womb.
From there began the world's springtime, the new year of history,
the year of joy and rest, of gladness and fullness – as the seventh
year was for the Hebrews, a year of gladness and rest, of suspen-
sion of work, of peace between everyone.[59] In being called, we
have been made part of that shoot which sprang up in Our Lady's
womb. "After saying this Jesus raised his eyes to heaven and said,
'Father, the hour has come. Glorify your Son so that the Son may
glorify You. Because You have given Him power over all flesh, so
that He might give eternal life to those You have given Him.'"[60]
The hour has come. This time is definitive. The hour we are living
is part of the hour that has come; the day that man will live tomorrow, the day after tomorrow, after one year, after a thousand,
ten thousand, years, is part of the hour that has come – the meaning of time is to glorify the Son, so that this Man, the incarnate
Son, might glorify the Father, reveal the Mystery of the Father,
make mankind's awareness penetrate more and more into the
Mystery that makes all things. So this Man, born of a woman,
died and risen, has received power over all flesh, without excep-
tion, so that "everyone" might have eternal life.

This "everyone" is not formed as a chaotic mass, but as a col-
umn of people that grows wider as time goes by. Christ clarified
the dynamics of this method He willed when He said, "You are
my friends, if you do what I command you. I do not call you ser-
vants, because the servant does not know what his master does,
but I have called you friends because everything I have heard
from the Father I have made known to you. You did not choose
me, but I have chosen you and constituted you so that you may
go and produce much fruit, fruit that will last."[61] The fruit is Jesus
Himself – that the world might know Him and follow Him.
Jesus speaks to some, to ten people or so. His whole lordship –
He was the plan of the universe and shortly after this He would
be consecrated Lord in His death and resurrection – is concentrated on a few whom He calls friends; what He loves coincides
with their heart, what He creates coincides with their works.

In this phrase of Jesus we feel the echo of the third chapter of Mark's Gospel, "He went up the hill, and *called to himself those he wanted* and they went to him. He appointed twelve to stay with Him and also to send to preach and to have power to cast out devils. So He appointed the twelve, Simon whom He named Peter, then James Son of Zebedee and John the brother of James, whom He named Boanerges, sons of thunder; and Andrew, Philip, Bartholomew, Matthew, Thomas, James, Son of Alphaeus, Thaddeus, Simon the Canaanite, and Judas Iscariot, the one who was to betray Him."[62] And here, one by one, follow all our names, too.

The Apostles and their successors enter with Christ into the flow of his Spirit and share in Jesus's own mission. Their fundamental function, the task they are chosen for, is to introduce mankind into a definitive relationship with the Mystery of God. And along with the bishops and the priests, all Christians are called to be part of this choice and of the responsibility for this function.[63]

"He called those he wanted"; "all flesh that the Father puts into his hands"; "those whom he wanted." This is the ontological foundation, the constituent factor of the Christian vocation as a task in the world. In first place lies the choice that Christ makes of us – choice, election. For human presumption and for present-day ideology, nothing is more irrational and anti-democratic than this word – "election," being chosen; but without this word there would be nothingness.

There was nothingness, the nothingness of everything, but more precisely your nothingness, my nothingness. The word "election" sets the limit, the boundary between nothingness and being. Being blossoms out of nothingness, as a choice, as election. There is no other condition that can be proposed, no other premise imaginable. This choice, this election, is the pure freedom of the Mystery of God in action, the absolute freedom of the Mystery that expresses itself.

The Mystery of God, which expresses itself in freedom of choice or in election, vibrates, it can and must vibrate, with fear and trembling, with absolute humility, in human preference, because human preference is the shadow of the choice of God's freedom.

But the choice of God's freedom, which chooses One, hidden like a tiny flower in Our Lady's womb, is for the whole world. So the humble echo of preference, full of fear and trembling, does not exist unless out of love for the world, for the benefit to be brought to the world, out of passion for the world. And how wonderful is this supreme paradox of a preference that chooses and elects so as to embrace the world, so as to draw the world along with itself. In making this preference, choice and election coincide with a love that fixes itself on every living person, on all flesh. "He has given him power over all flesh."[64] With the man He chooses and elects, Christ shares His power over all flesh.

3   BAPTISM: CONCEPTION AND BIRTH OF A NEW CREATURE

An objective fact

"You are all children of God through faith in Christ Jesus, because all of you who have been baptized in Christ, have put on Christ."[65] Christ's encounter with our life, in which He began to be a real event for us, His impact with our life, in which He moved towards us and, like a *vir pugnator*,[66] set off an "invasion" of our existence, is called Baptism. It is an objective fact: a man who is taken and passes through the water of a well, or of a fountain, as if he were passing through a sea, the sea of life. With this objective fact – that calls man to understand and accept to be part of the Event of Christ, for faith is part of the Event – a new man is born, a new people. Paul VI spoke of an ethnic entity *sui generis*:[67] this is the People that make history. The promise of which the Hebrew people, in their prophetic intuition, felt themselves to be the custodians, comes true here. With Baptism new people who make history are born.

In the hierarchy of values and interests that governs our life, there is normally nothing stranger than Baptism; yet nothing is more radically decisive for human existence than this fact called Baptism – a fact so real that its external effect can be wholly described: it has a precise date; it physically took hold of us in a given moment. Like any fact, it may appear to be something very fragile. Even Jesus walking through the fields or speaking in a town square could have seemed to be something very commonplace. But with that Event called Baptism, something irreducibly new began in us. It is a real Event that enters a situation and changes it, that determines it in a new way. This beginning, set in time, could eventually be buried under a thick blanket of earth or in a tomb of forgetfulness and ignorance. But every step of our journey to Destiny is anchored to that fact and must necessarily come back to it.

One with Christ

What does Baptism imply? You begin to understand it in a living Christian companionship, since in this companionship a memory is aroused that gives peace to the heart, satisfaction to the soul, and, at the same time, makes life combative, makes you realize that life is a battle for affirming Christ. So what does Baptism imply for me, what does it bring about? Baptism implies the participation of my person in the Mystery of Christ's person – my person is incorporated into the Mystery of Christ's person. The most relevant passage in this regard is from the *Letter to the Galatians*, "You who are baptized have become one with Christ."[68] Let's think about the meaning of the term "to become one with" when it is the case of one person who loves another person. A person who loves another and seeks to identify with that other has a terrible experience of being unable to penetrate into the other, of being ultimately a stranger. Not in the case of Christ! "Whoever is baptized has put on Christ, so there is no longer Jew nor Greek, slave or freeman, no male nor female, but you are all one, *eis*, one single person in Christ Jesus,"[69] the person of Christ Jesus. In the *Letter to the Romans* and in the letter to the Ephesians, St Paul goes as far as to say, "Don't you know that you are members one of another?"[70] This is the height which Christ has reached as Lord of history. In His Resurrection, He has set the terms of this assimilation to Himself, of this glory, of this making explicit that in Him all things consist, everything belongs to Him.[71] The assimilation to Christ brought about by Baptism is the Resurrection of Christ that penetrates history; it is the Body of the risen Christ that grows ever more according to the times of the Mystery of the Father. And the gesture that makes the journey of the new creature possible, the one re-made by the power of God and therefore capable of new things, is the Eucharist, *viaticum*, food for the journey, true nourishment for the person and for his hope. In this gesture, in giving Himself, Christ continues to bring man to perfection in Himself. Under the sign of matter, what the sign indicates really happens – Christ becomes one with me. An unimaginably profound ontological relationship is truly communicated to our life in a sign.[72]

The birth of a new creature

Baptism is the beginning of a new personality, of a "new creature"[73] in the world. If we think of the evident natural hierarchy of beings, in which a plant is more than a stone, an animal is more than a plant, and man is the summit of the hierarchy (as awareness of the need for happiness of which he, along with the whole world, is constituted), then Baptism creates a being that is greater, more human. It gives rise to a new creature.

The expression "new creature" is like a continuous refrain in the New Testament. For example in the *Second Letter to the Corinthians*, "So if anyone is in Christ, he is a new creature: the old things have passed away, and new things are here";[74] in the *Letter to the Galatians*, "What counts is not being circumcised or not being circumcised, but being a new creature";[75] in the *Letter to the Colossians*, "You have been stripped of the old man with his actions and have put on the new";[76] in the moving fourth chapter of the *Letter to the Ephesians*, "You must be renewed in the spirit of your minds and put on the new man."[77] St James speaks of Baptism as the beginning of a "new creation,"[78] and St Peter of a new generation, "not from a corruptible, but from an immortal seed."[79]

A novelty that contradicts the world

The new creature that is born with Baptism is contrary to what Christ defined as "the world." Of this He said, "Father, I pray

You for them, I do not pray for the world."[80] We are immersed in a "worldly" reality opposed to what has happened to us. This worldly reality needs the event of Christ, it needs it to be witnessed and lived, but as awareness and affection; it is radically foreign and opposed to the new personality, to the "new creature" to which Christ gives origin. "The time will come," says St Anthony of the desert, "in which men will go mad, and when they see someone who is not mad, they will turn against him and say, 'you are mad,' because he is not like them."[81]

Even those who are chosen can drown in the muddy ocean of the world, yielding to forgetfulness, not living the memory that is the awareness of Christ's presence, a real Event in the life of man. "This is the victory that overcomes the world, our faith,"[82] and our faith is the acknowledgment and the memory of that real Event that determines our life.

Now, the difference between being called in the objective gesture of Baptism and realizing what has happened (not in the sense of understanding but of perceiving the Mystery that reverberates in that moment and in that gesture), is marked by an "encounter." It is through an encounter that what we have been called to, what we have looked at respectfully, rather afraid and confused, begins to become clear, like the dawn that tinges the horizon with light. The encounter begins to shed a halo of light, a ray of light on something that has happened before. In this sense, the encounter is a source of memory, it awakens a memory that gives peace to your soul, like a hunger satisfied by food and a thirst quenched by a drink, and makes the whole body and the whole personality combative, in a present that changes.

4 THE COMPANIONSHIP GUIDED TOWARDS DESTINY IS A DIMENSION OF THE "I." – BELONGING

Recognizing being joined together in a companionship because Christ is there develops the sense of a belonging that constitutes the person himself. This kind of companionship is something substantial for the definition of our self. A person is not complete if not in companionship: a person generates companionship and is generated by a companionship. "Belonging" is the name of a relationship that goes this far – you belong to me and I belong to you; I belong to the companionship created by the Event of Christ, and this companionship, in its every factor, belongs to me and I to it.

The concrete companionship where the encounter with Christ takes place becomes the place of belonging of our self, from which it draws the ultimate way of perceiving and feeling things, the way of grasping them intellectually and of judging them, the way of imagining, planning, deciding, and doing. Our self belongs to this "Body," which is the Christian companionship, and from this it draws the ultimate criterion for tackling everything. Only this companionship, therefore, enables us to face reality, makes us touch reality and makes us real. With these words John Paul II described the interior dynamics that define the individual's relationship with the companionship: adhering to Christ "as the principle and inspiring motive for living and working, of awareness and action."[83]

Belonging to Christ is the content of a new self-awareness. We belong to God, we are His in the most radical and ontological sense of the word – we are His creatures, but our creaturely dependence would remain an enigmatic and fleeting perception if it had not been revealed clearly in Christ: "For no-one has seen God: the only-begotten Son who is in the bosom of the Father, has made Him known."[84] In belonging to the God who has become Man, our total dependence, our "being made," becomes clear. What defines me is an Other, I coincide with the will and the power of an Other, I belong to an Other, to Him who creates me. And He who creates me has become Man, so I am not what I think and feel about myself, but ultimately what this Man thinks and wants of me.

The companionship strikes us and we feel attracted because it makes the encounter with this Man a concrete experience. It takes away the abstraction and makes us experience it as a reality that we can live today. The companionship is not an idea, a discourse, a logic, but a fact, a presence that implies a relationship of belonging. Ideas, logic, consequentialities are then drawn from this belonging, but first one has to be within the fact of the companionship. The companionship demonstrates the Presence of God become man because it is made up of people who, if they remain faithful, eventually change. The belonging to the companionship, whatever form it takes, springs from an event, from an encounter from which comes a newness that begins in me, a new perception and adherence to myself. The beginning of a new creation springs up in me, one that cannot be ascribed to what I think or feel about myself.

In this belonging our whole person is taken up, and changes as time passes. We really think, perceive, judge, feel, and experience affection, work; in other words manipulate reality, give ourselves (our life, our death) in a profoundly different way, so much so that Jesus said to Nicodemus, "You have to be born again."[85] Ideas, discourses, and logic do not change a person. Being together with others, if it is consciously and freely adhered to, changes a person, and synthesizes all the factors, even in the most rebellious heart – provided it is not so rebellious as to go away. So begins a new creation of ourselves; that is to say, the discovery of the true creation.

In belonging, the person has the experience of a cohesion among the details that make up his life. Thus his life takes on a new meaning and a new unity. It is really a question of a new meaning, which cannot be reduced to the short breadth of time and space that we can measure. It is a meaning that goes infinitely beyond it. Only in the experience of this cohesion does there begin to dawn upon the horizon of our awareness the perception of a positive meaning of time, in spite of everything; in other words, of something greater and more powerful than evil and stronger than the narrowness of the present. Here we understand the value of the Christian companionship: it reminds us of where we are heading, of the meaning of what we are, of the profound beauty, of the tenacious tenderness; it reminds us of the intense capacity for sacrifice and dedication, all according to the ideal that springs from being assimilated to Christ in that moment, the greatest moment in life, which is called Baptism.

It is truly the Mystery of Christ that becomes present in the
Christian companionship and walks with us. In this new reality
a dynamism develops, which Péguy can help us to grasp:

"When the student does nothing but repeat not the same resonance, but a poor repetition of the master's thought; when the
student is no more than a student, even though he be the best
of all, he will never generate anything. A student does not begin
to create unless he introduces a new resonance (in other words
unless he is no longer a student). Not that he should not have a
master, but one must descend from the other by the natural ways
of fathering, not by the scholastic ways of discipleship."[86]

So this is the dynamism implied in belonging, this is the need
of a true companionship, so that it be the source of mission
throughout the whole world – not discipleship, not repetition,
but sonship. The introduction of a new reverberation, a new resonance is proper to a son, who has the father's own nature. He
has the same nature as the father, the same stock, but he is a new
reality. So much so that he can do better than the father, and the
father can look with delight on the son who has become greater
he is. But what the son does is greater precisely inasmuch as
he better realizes what he has seen and heard from the father.
Therefore, for the living, organic nature of the Christian companionship there is nothing more contradictory than, on the one
hand the affirmation of one's own opinion, of one's own measure, or one's own way of feeling as the ultimate criterion, and on
the other hand pure repetition. It is fathering that generates. The
blood of one, the father, passes into the heart of the other, the
son, and generates a new capacity for realization. Thus the great
Mystery of His Presence multiplies and spreads, so that all may
see Him and give glory to God.

The greatest sacrifice is to give your life
for the work of an Other

"Belonging" is the most important word for defining the nature
of the new creature through whom the ontology of the Event is
conveyed. So deepening the awareness of self as belonging is the

first line of development for a mature self-awareness; that is to say, for a Christian anthropology. The more the self perceives itself as belonging, the more it will give birth to actions whose form is correct and adequate to Destiny.

From the perception of the ontological value of belonging springs the moral formula that most intensely summarizes and indicates the way we live life: "The greatest sacrifice is to give your life for the work of an Other." This phrase is analogous to Christ's own, "Greater love has no man than this, that a man lay down his life for his friends."[87] But even more profoundly this phrase recalls – as does the whole of John's Gospel – Christ's own experience; Christ who gives His life for the work of the Father.

5 A NEW CONCEPTION OF INTELLIGENCE AND AFFECTION

To become a "new creature" means having a new awareness, a capacity for looking at and understanding reality that others cannot have, and a new affection, a capacity for adherence and dedication to reality, to what is other than oneself, one that cannot even be imagined. The "new creature" means an intelligence and a heart that are different in eating and drinking, in waking and sleeping, in living and in dying.[88] The words that in the Old Testament were bound to one's arms and written on the doorframes of the house become the normal consciousness in the "new creature," with which it passes through the whole web of circumstances that comprise reality: "In the experience of a great love ... everything becomes an event within its sphere."[89]

The new creature has a new *mens* (Greek: *nous*), a capacity for knowing reality that is different from everyone else's. How is this *nous* born? This new knowledge is born of the adherence to an event, from the affection for an event you have become attached to, that you have said *yes* to. This event is a particular detail in history. It has a universal claim, but it is a particular point. To take an event as a starting point for thought means first accepting that I am not the one who defines that event, but rather that the event defines me. What I really am and my conception of the world emerge in the event.[90] This is a challenge for the dominant mentality, which, when judging, always tends to subsume the particulars into an abstract universal. The new mentality, instead, is not born of a process of analytic deduction from certain principles or criteria that are then applied, but is born of an event, of something that has happened and happens; it is not born from me, but from what I encounter. It is not some method I apply, but obedience to what I have met.

The new knowledge implies, therefore, being contemporary with the event that generates it and continuously sustains it. Since this origin is not an idea, but a place, a living reality, the new judgment is possible only in an on-going relationship with this reality; in other words with the human companionship that prolongs the initial Event in time. This companionship proposes the authentic Christian point of view. The Event continues in history, and with it the origin of the new judgment continues. Whoever favours his own analyses or his own deductions will ultimately adopt the world's way of looking at things, which tomorrow will be different from what it is today. Maintaining the original position in which the Event arouses the new knowledge is the only way we can relate to reality without preconceptions, according to all its factors. A judgment permanently open and without prejudices is, in fact, impossible for purely human efforts, but it is the only one that respects and exalts the dynamism of reason (which is openness to reality according to all its factors).

For the mentality to be truly new, its awareness of "belonging" needs to be continually engaged in a comparison with present events. Since it is born of a place in the present, it judges the present, otherwise it is non-existent. If it does not enter into present experience, the new knowledge doesn't exist – it is an abstraction. In this sense, not to judge events is to mortify the faith.

The way in which the criterion for judging is born can be summed up in the word *gaze*. It is a matter of facing the event you have encountered, without at some point compromising the sincerity of your eyes out of concern for affirming your own liking or "interest." It is sincerity in looking at the event that gives us the new criterion of judgment, and saves us from yielding to the criteria of the "world," like a child before reality, who does not invent anything, and does not allow any other concern to enter into his gaze. As he grows, he will tend to look at the same thing while inserting factors that alter it, foreign factors that make the judgment insincere. He will adopt "worldly" criteria, whereas it is sincerity in looking at the event that makes for growth. It is an *affectus* such as Simon had, so purely and deeply filled with affection for Jesus, one that develops our capacity to judge reality adequately.

The same dynamics are expressed by St Paul in an enthusiastic phrase, "Though living in the flesh, I live in the faith of the Son of God, who loved me and gave himself for me."[91] This "for me" reaches out to the whole world and tries to embrace the whole world so that everyone may understand it. "Though living in the flesh ..." To live Christianity we are not asked to give up anything, but to change our way of relating with everything ("even the hairs on your head are numbered");[92] "you will be held to account for every idle word."[93] "Though living in the flesh," that is to say, in the situation as it is – before the girl who attracts me, in a family where the mother and father are always fighting, working twelve hours a day, sick, unable to do all you have to, distracted, forgetful – "I live in faith in the Son of God." In other words, I belong to an Event, to an origin that changes the way I look at things; the way I look at things becomes faith. Living in the flesh, I am part of an Event that makes me capable of a new intelligence, a more profound and truer understanding of my circumstances.[94] What does it mean to look at a girl's face according to the flesh? It means that it's all just a matter of whether I like her or not, whether she's to my taste or not, whether I find her hard or easy to be with. Whereas "Though living in the flesh, I live in faith" means I approach my relationship with her in faith in the Son of God, in my adherence to Christ. So that girl, insofar as she is attractive, is the sign through which I am invited to adhere in the flesh to the being of things, to get down to the reality of things, right down to where they are made.[95] There is no greater evidence, there is nothing more evident for a man who uses his reason, than the fact that in this instant, in this moment,

I am not making myself. I am You who are making me, I am an Other who makes me. The Mystery of God who generates me has come down so near to me as to reveal His identity with my form, with my being, with my consistency. St Paul says, "I am living, not I, but You are living in me."[96] There is a relationship with the Mystery who makes all things, there is a relationship with the Mystery become flesh, become man, Jesus, that is immensely more human, more mine, more immediate, more tenacious, more tender, more unavoidable than the relationship with anyone else – with my mother, my father, my fiancée, my wife, my children – with everyone and with everything. For everything is born from the Mystery, nothing makes itself. This is why the person before me, whoever he may be, *is* and marks out the road through which I reach Christ, the You of which all things are made, and so for that person I have esteem, respect, adoration, I can adore his face. But I adore this face if it is the road towards the source of all things, the source of Being. Otherwise it is like drawing a figure without perspective, it is an infantile, primitive, perception.

"Though living in the flesh, I live in faith in the Son of God." This is the definition of the profound change of man's intelligence and expression. I go beyond, to the root of the face of things and reach the point in which the thing is an Other that makes it, the You that makes it, Christ. The divine coincides thus with the ultimate consistency of reality, of man.[97]

6 A NEW MORALITY

To speak of the new understanding of reality, introducing the concept of *affectus*, means to reach the threshold of the moral problem. New knowledge and new morality have the same origin. For Simon, son of John, and for Paul, the origin of the new knowledge is identical to the origin of their new morality – a present Event.

Out of one's belonging to the companionship of Christ a new conception of the moral problem is born. In the confusion, the dark loneliness, and the whirling violence that dominate our world today, everyone speaks of morality, but the problem never emerges in its truth. A man's act is moral when it takes account of the whole. An act is true, moral, only if it corresponds to the overall plan; if it leaves out some part, then it is no longer moral. It is analogous to the dynamism of reason. Reason is awareness of reality according to all its factors; if it leaves out just one of them, then it is no longer reason, but falsehood. Analogously, an act is moral when it maintains its original openness to reality with which God continuously creates us.

The corruption of morality that is particularly fashionable these days is called moralism. Moralism is the unilateral choice of values to justify one's own view of things. Normally people understand that without a certain order one cannot conceive of life, reality, or existence. But how do they define this order? Considering reality according to the various points of view they start from, they describe it in its stable dynamics and draw up a list of principles and laws, the fulfillment of which, they believe, will create order. In this way, age after age, the various analytical propositions in which human reflection outlines its claims take shape: "You have to do this and that." The Pharisees defined order with a seemingly endless number of laws. From a certain point of view the Pharisee is a man who likes order; the defender of morality understood as that order affirmed and outlined in all its details as far as humanly possible.

Moralism has two grave symptoms. The first is pharisaism. No one is more contrary to the Gospel than someone who considers himself honest,[98] because he has no need of Christ. The Pharisee lives without any tension, because he himself establishes the measure of what is right and he identifies it with what he thinks he is capable of. As a defence, he uses violence against anyone who is not like him. So the second symptom is readiness to lie. On the one hand he justifies himself, and on the other hand he hates and condemns his neighbour. But there is one further consequence of what we have said. There can be many different moralities, and the intentions that form them can all seem just in theory, but man is impotent before the ideals that he himself lays down as a path to follow on his journey.

Who is capable of morality? In his weakness, every man is
a sinner. If we lack the awareness of being sinners we cannot
approach anyone without injustice, presumption, pretension,
aggression, calumny, and falsehood. Awareness of being sinners
makes us capable of discretion, keen on the truth for ourselves
and for others, hopeful that at least the other might be better
than oneself, and humble. We cannot establish any true relationship unless we begin from the awareness of being sinners, of
what we lack and of where we fail.

This is the point which Christ returned to insistently, as the
prophets had done before him. What man can say, "I am obedi-
ent to all the laws"? One can say, "I acknowledge that these laws
are necessary," but who keeps them all? Who can say, "I keep
them all"? The Pharisee in the temple! But he is a Pharisee; the
very meaning of the word has altered and become synonymous
with impostor or hypocrite. Meanwhile at the back of the temple
we find the poor tax-collector who admits he has gone against
the law, "Lord, have mercy on me, a sinner."[99]

Coherence is a miracle, so true morality is a miracle. It is in
faithfulness to the Christian companionship that, with time, a
person finds himself becoming capable of things that he could
never have imagined: "Yours, Lord, is the grace."[100]

In the kingdom of God, there is no measure. "Let no-one judge,
because only God is the judge."[101] St Paul also says, "I judge no-
one, not even myself."[102] Only God measures all the factors of
the man who acts, and his measure is beyond all measure – it
is called mercy, something which for us is ultimately incomprehensible. As the man Jesus said of those who were killing him,
"Father, forgive them for they don't know what they are doing."[103] Christ built up their defence on the tiny margin of their
ignorance. Our imitation of Christ is in the margin of mercy.

For this reason morality is striving, starting over and over
again. Like a child who is learning to walk: he can fall ten times,
but he keeps going towards his mother, he gets up and keeps going. Evil does not stop us. We can fall a thousand times, but evil
does not define us, as it defines the present-day mentality, which
has people ultimately justify what they cannot avoid doing. A

characteristic of true morality, therefore, is the desire for correction. The term "correction" that translates the Latin "*regere cum,*" to walk supporting each other.

A final symptom of morality as "tending to" is the absence of scandal. A Christian who lives the companionship is not scandalized at anything; he feels sorrow for evil, but is not scandalized.

How did this new morality enter the world? How did it appear?

"Simon, do you love me?"

The twenty-first chapter of John's Gospel is a fascinating documentation of the historical birth of the new ethic. The particular story narrated there is the keystone of the Christian conception of man, of his morality, in his relationship with God, with life, and with the world. The disciples were on their way back, at dawn, after a terrible night's fishing on the lake, in which they had caught nothing. As they approach the shore, they see a figure on the beach preparing a fire. Later they would notice that there were some fish on the fire collected for them, for their early-morning hunger. All of a sudden, John says to Peter, "That's the Lord!" They all open their eyes and Peter throws himself into the water, just as he is, and reaches the shore first. The others follow suit. They sit down in a circle in silence; no one speaks, because they all know it is the Lord. Sitting down to eat, they exchange a few words, but they are all fearful at the exceptional presence of Jesus, the Risen Jesus, who had already appeared to them at other times.

Simon, whose many errors had made him humbler than all the others, sat down, too, before the food prepared by the Master. He looks to see who is next to him and is terrified to see that it is Jesus Himself. He turns his gaze away from Him and sits there, all embarrassed. But Jesus speaks to him. Peter thinks in his heart, "My God, My God, what a dressing-down I deserve! Now he is going to ask me, 'Why did you betray me?' " The betrayal had been the last great error he had made, but, in spite of his familiarity with the Master, his whole life had been a stormy one, because of his impetuous character, his instinctive stubbornness, his tendency to act on impulse. He now saw himself in the light of all his defects. That betrayal had made him more aware of all his other errors, of the fact that he was worthless, weak, miserably weak. "Simon." – who knows how he must have trembled as that word sounded in his ears and touched his heart? – "Simon" – here he would have begun to turn his face towards Jesus – "do you love me?" Who on earth would have expected that question? Who would have expected those words?

Peter was a forty- or fifty-year-old man, with a wife and children, and yet he was such a child before the mystery of that companion he had met by chance! Imagine how he felt transfixed by that look that knew him through and through. "You will be called *Kefas*."[104] His tough character was described by that word "rock," and the last thing he had in mind was to imagine what the mystery of God and the mystery of that Man – the Son of God – had to do with that rock, to that rock. From the first encounter, He filled his whole mind, his whole heart. With that presence in his heart, with the continuous memory of Him, he looked at his wife and children, his work-mates, friends and strangers, individuals and crowds, he thought, and he fell asleep. That Man had become for him like an immense revelation, still to be clarified.

"Simon, do you love me?" "Yes, Lord, I love You." How could he say such thing after all he had done? That *yes* was an affirmation acknowledging a supreme excellence, an undeniable excellence, a sympathy that overwhelmed all others. Everything remained inscribed in that look. Coherence or incoherence seemed to fall into second place behind the faithfulness that felt like flesh of his flesh, behind the form of life which that encounter had moulded. In fact, no reproof came, only the echo of the same question: "Simon, do you love me?" Not uncertain, but fearful and trembling, he replied again, "Yes, I love You." But the third time, the third time that Jesus threw the question at him, he had to ask confirmation from Jesus Himself: "Yes, Lord, You know I love You." All my human preference is for You, all the preference of my mind, all the preference of my heart; You are the extreme preference of life, the supreme excellence of things. I don't know,

I don't know how, I don't know how to say it and I don't know how it can be but, in spite of all I have done, in spite of all I can still do, I love You.

This *yes* is the birth of morality, the first breath of morality in the dry desert of instinct and pure reaction. Morality sinks its roots into this Simon's *yes*, and this *yes* can take root in man's soil only thanks to a dominant Presence, understood, accepted, embraced, served with all the energy of your heart; only in this way can man become a child again. Without a Presence, there is no moral act, there is no morality. But why is Simon's *yes* to Jesus the birth of morality? Don't the criteria of coherence and incoherence come first?

Peter had done just about all the wrong he could do, yet he lived a supreme sympathy for Christ. He understood that everything in him tended to Christ, that everything was gathered in those eyes, in that face, in that heart. His past sins could not amount to an objection, nor even the incoherence he could imagine for the future. Christ was the source, the place of his hope. Had someone objected to what he had done or what he might have done, Christ remained, through the gloom of those objections, the source of light for his hope. And he esteemed Him above everything else, from the first moment in which he had felt himself stared at by His eyes, looked on by Him. This is why he loved Him. "Yes, Lord, you know You are the object of my supreme sympathy, of my highest esteem." This is how morality is born. The expression is very generic: "Yes, I love You." But it is as generic as it is generative of a new life to be lived.

"Whoever has this hope in Him purifies himself as He is pure."[105] Our hope is in Christ, in that Presence that, however distracted and forgetful we be, we can no longer (not completely anyway) remove from the earth of our heart because of the tradition through which He has reached us. It is in Him that I hope, before counting my errors and my virtues. Numbers have nothing to do with this. In the relationship with Him, numbers don't count, the weight that is measured or measurable is irrelevant, and all the evil I can possibly do in the future has no relevance either. It cannot usurp the first place that this *yes* of Simon, repeated by me, has before the eyes of Christ. So a kind of flood comes from the depths of our heart, like a breath that rises from the breast and pervades the whole person, making it act, making it want to act more justly. The flower of the desire for justice, for true, genuine love, the desire to be capable of acting gratuitously, springs up from the depths of the heart. Just as our every move starts off not from an analysis of what the eyes see, but from an embrace of what the heart is waiting for, in the same way perfection is not the keeping of rules, but adhesion to a Presence.

Only the man who lives this hope in Christ lives the whole of his life in ascesis, in striving for good. And even when he is clearly contradictory, he desires the good. This always conquers, in the sense that it is the last word on himself, on his day, on what he does, on what he has done, on what he will do in the future. The man who lives this hope in Christ keeps on living in ascesis. Morality is a continual striving towards "perfection" that is born of an event that is a *sign* of a relationship with the divine, with the Mystery.

The ultimate reason for the yes

What is the true reason for the *yes* that Simon answers to Christ? Why does the *yes* said to Christ matter more than listing all your errors and the possible future errors that your weakness forebodes? Why is this *yes* more decisive and greater than all the moral responsibility expressed in its details, in concrete practice? The answer to this question reveals the ultimate essence of the One sent by the Father. Christ is the One "sent" by the Father; He is the One who reveals the Father to men and to the world. "This is true life: that they may know You, the only true God, and the one You have sent, Jesus Christ."[106] The most important thing is that "they know You," that they love You, because this You is the meaning of life.

"Yes, I love You," Peter said. And the reason for this *yes* consisted in the fact that in those eyes that had set on him that first time, and had set on him so many other times during the following days and years, he had glimpsed who God was, who Yahweh

was, the true Yahweh: *mercy*.[107] God's relationship with his creature is revealed in Jesus as love, and therefore as mercy. Mercy is
the attitude of the Mystery towards any kind of weakness, error,
and forgetfulness on man's part: in the face of any crime that
man commits, God loves him. Simon felt this. This is where his
"Yes, I love You" comes from.

The meaning of the world and of history is the mercy of Christ,
Son of the Father, sent by the Father to die for us. In Milosz's
play *Miguel Mañara* Miguel was going to the Abbot every day to
weep over his past sins. One day the Abbot tells him, somewhat
impatiently, "Stop weeping like a woman. All this never existed."
What does he mean by "never existed"? Miguel had murdered,
raped, he had done all kinds of things. "All this never existed.
Only He is."[108] He, Jesus, addresses us, becomes an "encounter"
for us, asking us only one thing: not "What have you done?" but
"Do you love me?"

To love Him above all things, then, does not mean that I have
not sinned or that I will not sin tomorrow. How strange! It takes
an infinite power to be this mercy, an infinite power from which
– in this world, in the time and space given to us to live, whether
for few or many years – we obtain, we draw gladness. Because,
in the awareness of all his lowliness, a man is happy at the announcement of this mercy. Jesus is mercy. He is sent by the Father
to let us know that the supreme feature of the essence of God for
man is mercy. "You have bent down over our wounds and have
healed us," says a Preface in the Ambrosian liturgy, "giving us a
medicine stronger than our scars, a mercy greater than our fault.
Thus even sin, in virtue of your invincible love, served to raise us
up to divine life."[109] From this gladness comes peace, comes the
possibility of peace. We, too, in all our misfortunes, in all our evil
deeds, in all our incoherence, in all our weakness, in that mortal
weakness that man is, can really breathe and long for peace, and
generate peace and respect for others.

Respecting the other means looking at him with your eye on
another Presence. The second century *Letter to Diognetus* says,
"The Christians treat each other with a respect inconceivable
to others."[110] The word "respect" (*respectus*, from *re-spicio*) has

the same root as *aspicio* (to look) and the *re-* indicates that you keep your eyes directed at something, like someone who is walking along while keeping his eyes on the object he is approaching. "Respect" means "looking at a person while keeping another in mind." It is like looking after a child when the mother is nearby: a teacher does not treat the child as she normally might, assuming she has some sense of modesty (perhaps even this is lost today). Without respect for what I make use of, for what is there for my use, for what I take hold of because I need it, there is no adequate relationship with anything. But respect cannot derive from the fact that I need what I have before me. From this point of view I merely dominate it. No, respect gives a "background" to what I use. Thus work becomes something noble and light-hearted, amidst all the worries we get up with in the morning. And our morning prayer is the renewal of this awareness. A man who looks at his wife while perceiving and acknowledging the Other, Jesus, within and beyond his wife's role and form, can have respect and veneration for her, can respect her freedom, which is relationship with the infinite, relationship with Jesus.

The beginning of human morality is an act of love

Simon's *yes* to Jesus cannot be considered the expression of a mere feeling; it is the beginning of a moral road that either opens with that *yes* or does not open at all. The beginning of a human morality is not the analysis of the phenomena that fill the self's existence, nor the analysis of human behaviour in view of a common good; this could be the beginning of an abstract secular morality, but not of a human morality.

St Thomas notes, "Man's life consists in the affection that chiefly sustains him and in which he finds the greatest satisfaction."[111] The beginning of human morality is an act of love. This requires a presence, the presence of someone who strikes us, who gathers all our powers and stirs them, attracting them to a good that is unknown, but is desired and awaited, that good which is Mystery.

The dialogue between Jesus and Peter ends in a strange way. Peter, who is about to follow Jesus, is concerned about the youngest, John, who was like a son to him. "And seeing him, he said to Jesus, 'What of him, Lord?' Jesus replies, 'Do not worry about him, just follow me.'"[112] That *yes* is directed to a Presence that says, "Follow me, leave your life behind." "*Jesu, tibi vivo, Jesu, tibi morior, Jesu, sive vivo sive morior, tuus sum.*"[113] Whether you live or die you are mine. You belong to me. I made you. I am your destiny. I am your meaning and the meaning of the world.

The protagonist of morality is the whole person, the whole "I." And the person has for its law a word that we all think we know and whose meaning, after a long time, if we are minimally faithful to what is original in us, we begin to glimpse: the word is love. The person has love for its law. "God, Being, is love," St John writes.[114]

Love is a judgment that is "moved" because of a Presence connected to destiny. It is a judgment, such as when you say, "This is Mont Blanc," or "This is a friend of mine." Love is a judgment filled with emotion because of a Presence connected with my destiny, that I discover; I glimpse, I sense that I am connected with my destiny. When John and Andrew saw Him for the first time and heard Him say, "Come home with me. Come and see," and then spent all those hours listening to Him talking, they didn't understand, but they sensed that that person was connected with their destiny. They had heard all the public speakers, all their opinions and all the party slogans. But only that man was connected with their destiny. Christian morality is a revolution on earth, because it is not a list of laws, but love for being. You can do wrong a thousand times and you will always be forgiven, you will always be picked up and you can start your journey again, if your heart takes up that *yes* again. What is important in that "Yes, Lord, I love You" is a striving of my whole person, determined by the awareness that Christ is God and by love for this Man who came for me. My whole awareness is determined by this, and I can go wrong a thousand times a day, and be afraid to lift up my head, but no one can take this certainty from me. I just pray the Lord, pray the Spirit to change me, to make me an imitator of Christ, so that my presence may become more like the presence of Christ himself.

Morality is love, it is love for Being become man, an event in history, that reaches me through the mysterious companionship that historically is called the Church, or the mysterious Body of Christ, or the People of God: I love Him in this companionship. I can be scolded for a hundred thousand errors, they can take me to court, the judge can send me to prison even without a trial, with blatant injustice, without asking whether or not I am guilty, but they cannot take this attachment from me, which keeps thrilling me with the desire for good; in other words, attachment to Him. Because the good is not "the good," but attachment to Him, following that face, His Presence, carrying His Presence everywhere, telling it to anyone and everyone, so that this Presence may dominate the world; for the end of the world will be the moment in which this Presence becomes evident to everyone.

This is the new morality. It is a love, not rules to follow. And evil is to offend the object of love or to forget it. You could humbly analyze all the pathways of a man's life, and could quite rightly say, "this is bad, this is good," make a list of all the errors a man can make and put them in order, and then you would have a textbook on morality. But morality is in me, morality is that I love Him who made me and is here present. If this weren't the case I could use morality exclusively for pressing my own advantage, and in any case it would lead to despair. You have to read the works of Pasolini or Pavese to understand this. But, there again, on the other hand, you only need to remember Judas.

The permanence of the new morality

If the beginning of the new morality is an act of love, of adherence, and this requires the Presence of someone who has struck us and attracted all our powers – just as Jesus did to Simon – then we have to answer the question of how this event goes on living as a presence in our day-to-day existence. The answer establishes the possibility of the new morality in the present, here and now, otherwise it would begin for us as something intellectual, abstract, and discursive. This answer lies in that Christian word that belongs to the experience of the present, without which we could not even know whether our experience is concrete or just fantasy. The word is "memory." In memory, the event that I experience in all its wealth becomes immersed in the flow of time and space, it is part of a history.

The first condition for a new morality is to live the memory of that Presence, which is beyond the bounds of human knowledge, i.e., to acknowledge, here and now, the Presence that cannot be reduced to any human hypothesis. This Presence is a reality that stands before us and, by the power of His Spirit, is in us. It is permanent in our life, and is so powerful that, in our adherence to it, it makes a new creation possible in us. So, after imperfection and error, at the end of every action, which is always out of proportion and always imperfect, you can get up again and do better, because His gift goes on, like a fresh spring, which no limitation of ours can stop.

The permanence of this Presence is grace, pure event, and we cannot resist adhering to it here and now. We acknowledge it and adhere to it. It is grace, as is the encounter, the astonishment, its continuity and the impulse of adherence. And this grace becomes ours because we accept it. Accepting this absolute newness, which happens over and over again a thousand times a day, is the supreme aspect of freedom. Just as for John and Andrew, for Simon, for Zacchaeus, the beginning of our change is a grace, a gift. We have had an encounter whose aim is to change us and fulfill us, and we have adhered to this Presence, which corresponds exceptionally to our expectations, with a lasting adherence, as for Zacchaeus, who was no longer determined by the imperfection he fell into, because that Presence was there like a pure, cool stream, washing away the filth from the forest of his humanity.[115]

The awe of the encounter, the permanence of that awe, the adherence to that Presence that goes on, imply the embrace and the unity with all those whom the Presence itself puts near us. This Presence is set before our eyes so that through us, with our defects, and our sorrow for these defects, and the strange impetus it gives, it may be more known and loved.

7 RESPONSIBILITY AND DECISION

We have been loved and we are loved; this is why we "are." The moral law and morality, in other words the concrete lack of proportion, expressed in action, of our person to the mystery of Being, are judged by this first and fundamental "law": acknowledging and accepting to be loved. We are loved. As a consequence it follows that loving, in its essential form, in its supreme expression, is accepting to be loved, because all the rest flows from here.

If I am loved, if I "am" because I am loved, then the great problem of my existence, of my being in the world, what makes it possible for my subject to become protagonist of a new world, in which the eternal begins to be experienced in time, is my answer – *my answer to the You* that loves me, my correspondence, my valuing of what He created in me at my origin, precisely so that I could become aware of Him, of Him who, in an exceptional way, decided to come amongst us, to live with me and to speak to me in a familiar way with His words, not copied from the dictionary, but drawn from the eternal, from the depths of Being in which he has made me share.

If I am because I am loved, I have to respond (*respondeo*): this is the origin of "responsibility." This is the endpoint of all the passionate emotion of our being, loaded with an eternal sensitivity, in movement towards the moulding of the final form, which is the glory of Christ's face,[116] in which even the smallest pebble will have its place.[117] It is the word "responsibility" that assures the outcome of an experience of correspondence with the truth, with the fascination of beauty, with the moving experience of the good, with ineffable happiness. In its completeness, the greatness of the word "responsibility" is the main source of zest for life. If you are not responsible within what gives you pleasure or what attracts you, if you do not participate in it with some responsibility, then it is not yours. So heaven implies a decision of yours, it implies responsibility, because heaven is for man and man is free.[118]

Responsibility is expressed as freedom's decision in front of the Presence that is acknowledged as corresponding totally to one's destiny. But all too often our way of thinking of freedom's decision is mistaken, as if it were an act I ultimately determine, as if I were the one to decide to answer *yes* to you and to decide to say, "your will be done." No, it is something else. The decision cannot be taken in the voluntary sense (as being synonymous with willpower).

To understand its dynamics let's think of the tax-collector at the back of the temple: he didn't dare raise his eyes, he just said, "Lord have mercy on me!" and he sensed that his request would be accepted, that God would appreciate it and that justice was thus satisfied.[119] And let's think of St Peter again.[120] Why, when Christ asked him, "Do you love me?" was not even the betrayal of a few days earlier an obstacle? He answered *yes* at once, as the consequence of an awe that had begun at Capernaum, when Andrew, his brother, had brought him to Christ and he had felt himself looked at by Him in such a way as to be transfixed and defined in his humanness, in his character, so much so that he had his name changed.[121] What was that exceptional impression, that initial awe made of, even psychologically speaking? The initial awe was a judgment that at once became an attachment. It was a judgment that stuck like glue, a judgment that affixed Peter and the disciples to Him like glue. As each day passed, it added another "coat of glue," and they could no longer free themselves. "But you never obey the laws!"[122] All the Pharisees were scandalized by their Master because He went around with those who didn't keep the laws! And the apostles didn't know what to answer: "We don't know if we are obeying the laws or not, but we are attached to this man." It was not a sentimental attachment, an emotional phenomenon, but a phenomenon of reason, a manifestation of that reason that "attaches" you to the person before you, since it is a judgment of value. As you look at the person you are taken up by a wonder full of esteem that attaches you to him. There is no hint of irrationality or forcing. "If we go away from You where shall we go? You have the words that explain life," Peter told Him one day, impetuous as always.[123] And after that affirmation he got it all wrong again, so much so that Jesus told him "Go away from me Satan! Because you don't want me to do what my Father wants, but what you have in mind."[124] What a humiliation! But the outcome was that Peter became even more attached to Him.

Peter's *yes* was neither the result of willpower nor the result of a "decision" of Simon, the man. It was the emergence, the surfacing of a whole chain of tenderness and of adherence that was explained by the esteem he had for Him (therefore it was an act of reason), which meant his only answer could be *yes*. This is the truest, the most genuine human "mechanism," that which makes us better friends of those who are friends to us, that fills us with tenderness for our mother and admiration for our father. It increases with time, and never stops. And it is not irrational; it is the only thing that is rational. For Peter, it was a friendship that did not depend on him, but had been brought to birth in him. For many would listen to Jesus and say "wonderful," but then they would go away. This friendship, this tenderness did not take root in them.

It was not a decision as we normally conceive of it, which is to say as the only way in which freedom goes into action. The nature of the decision is not a strong act of will as in Alfieri's "Want, always want, want with all your might!"[125] Man is fragile and as weak as a child.[126] Only if man acknowledges this does he begin to grow. So the decision springs forth as the establishment of a sympathy. The apostles followed Jesus because they were attached to Him with a judgment that made them capable of a perfectly rational decision, because where a relationship is generated that turns into a deep sympathy, when an attachment born of an incomparable awe is renewed, rationality is an event.[127]

8 THE CONCRETE FORM OF THE ELECTION IS THE TEMPLE IN TIME

The new self is born in Christ's gesture of choosing, which places it within the human companionship generated by His Spirit, i.e., into the Church. This election, this choice, always takes on a concrete historical form.

Christ takes hold of man in Baptism; He makes him grow and become an adult. And in an encounter He causes him to experience the fact that a new human reality is close to him, one that corresponds, convinces, educates, and is creative, and that strikes him in some way. Then the person says, "I'll go along with them"; in other words he decides to accept the prompting that he has felt, which spurs him towards the human reality he has encountered. He accepts it because he is struck by something, be it only a whisper, for the Lord works even through whispers: "Then the LORD passed by. There was a strong and powerful wind enough to shatter the mountains and split the rocks before the LORD, but the LORD was not in the wind. After the wind there was an earthquake, but the LORD was not in the earthquake. After the earthquake there was a fire, but the LORD was not in the fire. After the fire there was the whisper of a gentle wind."[128] The LORD was in the whisper of that gentle wind.

Even in a whisper, even just for a moment, man notices a kind of attraction, a suggestion; he has the intuition of something more beautiful, more correspondent, something better. And he says *yes*. The encounter could have been with a hundred thousand other temperaments or other human fascinations, but for him it was this one. He met a particular companionship and perceived the new whisper of a promise of life; he sensed a Presence that corresponded to the original expectation of his heart. So this is the companionship, not another one, in which Christ has become a companion for his life, and draws close to him on the journey. In this companionship he can repeat the greatest, the most wonderful words, "My soul clings to you, your right hand holds me fast."[129]

The Mystery of God, which otherwise would have seemed very distant and abstract, thus becomes something stirring in everyday life, an invitation to look at the sky and the earth, an emotion and a passion in opening one's heart to a preference, a preference that is true if it opens you up to the need of the whole world, thus sharing in the great love of Christ. Because the great love of Christ blossomed in the world through preferences: for John, for Simon ... But it would not have been a true preference if it had not been the sign of the great new love of Christ for the whole world.

The companionship that you meet with has certain characteristics, and it is because of an encounter with particular characteristics, with a particular accent, with a particular attraction, with a particular shape, that you find yourself there.

Man's dwelling place

God reveals Himself to His creature in time and space, and therefore in humanly understandable terms. God's Mystery, as Mystery, is irresistibly communicated to man.[130] This statement has an absolutely paradoxical feature. Christ, as the meaning of all time and all history, enters into communication with man, He reveals Himself, in a point of time and space. Through contingent and definitively given circumstances, He specifies what man is called to hear, know, acknowledge, and witness of the familiar choice to which God binds Himself and conditions the relationship with Him. These circumstances imply a place in which God asks of man that all be centred and operate as a sign of His relationship with man and man's with Him, and that all be totally a function of God's will in history. In the bible, this place is called "dwelling place," "home," "temple." The temple is the place where man meets the companionship of the Lord, where he hears His voice and His message. It is the place where the Lord points the way, the stretch of the road that He wants to show, where everything (the companionship amongst men and with things) recalls the nearness of Destiny. This is the answer to the ultimate need of man's reason, expressed by Moses: "Show me your face; if You do not come with us we will not move from here."[131]

An Other led us to what is decisive for bringing us into the secure and definitive relationship with our Destiny. And the form of this encounter is a precise companionship whose beginning and development can be given a date, with a face that distinguishes it from all other companionships. Just as a father – "a good father," Péguy would say – tries to make the proposal to his son more agreeable, as well-suited to him as possible.

This companionship established for us by Christ's Spirit has a structure, a framework, precise parameters that define it.

This basic parameter for building the structure of this companionship is the "home" or "dwelling place." A dwelling place is like the coalescence of the companionship, of the community, of charity, in a real, day-to-day, spatial dimension. It is from this home that everything starts off, that everything can start off in a new way; everything is made to grow, put in order, reinforced, made more affecting. Everything becomes love. The person you meet along the road, the person you meet in your apartment-block become possible objects of love, the person you knock against in the train, as well as the people with whom you share that place and that activity that for too many is senseless – daily work. Everything can become the object of love starting off from this dwelling place.

The great dwelling place that is the Church becomes flesh, is realized in capillary terminals (just as your veins end in tiny capillaries), in which it becomes present in every place, chosen beforehand by God's plan. The great dwelling place that is the Church is realized inside homes, the dwelling places that are the concentration, the coalescence of her life in a day-to-day dimension of space and time.

This dwelling place can take two forms:

a) Family
This is the home of those who are called to set up a family and therefore to form the generative instrument that produces the subject of all historical activity, the protagonist of God's plan – man. This is the normal vocation, without which history would come to an end – the family, the root of the perennial development of history, home of Jesus, dwelling place of the Son of man. The family is an original sign, given by the Creator himself. For the most decisive instrument for introducing us into the definitive relationship with destiny, and therefore even now to truth, to beauty, and to justice in the relationship with any thing or person, is pre-established, but not by us. We are not the ones to decide. An Other establishes this instrument; He who gives our

nature the urge for mutual esteem and gratuitousness which is part of our makeup, He is the one who created the first form of experience, which will remain throughout history, a place where this urge for charity becomes stable and essential – the family.

The companionship between man and woman exists for the generation of a people. A man and a woman get married; this gesture means that each identifies in the other the sign of the relationship with the whole, with the meaning of everything, given by God to his or her life. The encounter between man and woman cannot be defined exclusively by the aim of having children, but first and foremost by being companionship to Destiny, as the realization of the fundamental aim of every kind of human companionship. This bond, therefore, becomes the example for every other companionship. The very form of community life of those who dedicate their lives to God finds its inspiration in this ideal of the family. And those who live as a family, in their turn, find in those who are dedicated to God an example in practice, full of suggestion and encouragement for themselves, of the totality of this ideal.

As it happens, historically, God wills the continuity of that initial companionship between man and woman and He makes them father and mother. Thus a man and a woman cannot establish a stable relationship and be a companionship to Destiny for each other unless they are ready to collaborate in the plan God has for the world, in other words in creation, in the generation of a people that will run the whole course of history so as to flow out into the sea of Christ's definitive glory on the last day.

What is needed for a man and woman to become father and mother? First of all a new way of looking at each other. A man who looks at his wife only out of the tenderness she stirs up in him, or because she makes his heart beat faster, could procreate, could become a father in the merely biological sense, even unintentionally. But God, who is attentive, grasps even this first meaningless moment and immediately fills it with the meaning for which it is to be lived, of which it is made. Once the child is conceived, even a father who is totally unfeeling and hardhearted, after the first surprise, begins to reflect. He looks at his wife in a different way. Both look at each other differently. The first condition of this new way of looking at each other is the permanence, the essential bond, from which is extracted the fragrance of belonging. And here begins the best part: gratuitousness. From now on, even if the woman were to be unfaithful to the man, the man would forgive her and vice-versa. And above all, even were the man not to like the woman any more, the path would still be the same and the bond would last as before, even more perfectly, in other words more gratuitously. In this gratuitousness love is almost forced to squeeze into the narrow path through which it will flow out into charity. It is an Event that gives rise to this bond, just as a child gives a new beginning to a family. In the Event the stable bond emerges, the bond of belonging. Here life begins to be satisfied, to take delight in itself, in the right sense for a creature. There is a qualitative jump in the look between man and woman, where respect becomes possible (*re-spicere*), and the relationship becomes more and more meaningful as a sign of totality; in other words as a sign of collaboration with the Kingdom of God. The awareness of sharing in the building of the Kingdom of God introduces a new vibration into the soul, so that the loving feeling – through a tremendously narrow path called the cross – becomes genuine charity, virginity, gratuitousness; in other words, charity as participation in virginity, since virginity is the whole of life lived in the acknowledgment that Christ is everything in everyone.[132]

b) *The Monastery*

The second mode of dwelling place is the monastery. This is the word that is etymologically most meaningful amongst all the words that indicate the "dwelling place" of those who are called to virginity as their form of life. The word monastery comes from *monos* (alone, solitary); for mankind's relationship with God, with the Mystery, becomes awareness, freedom, and love in the individual person. It becomes a new self. But "monastery" means many selves who live together. Even the example of the hermit is a provisional one that does not make the rule: all these *monoi*, in one way or another, express and document their being all one in the Church of God by joining together. The other word, analogous to the word monastery, is "convent" (joining together).

The monastery, convent, or as the expression of a new form of dedication to God, "house,"[133] according to the various modes of the call, is made, created, built by those who are chosen as "living stones"[134] to form, to generate an existence that can be experienced by everyone, which demonstrates by its very visible form that "only He is." In the monastery, in the convent, or in the house, these living stones, those who are called and chosen, are there to demonstrate in virginity, in the very form of their life, that only He is; in other words, that Christ is the King of the Universe (*Christe cunctorum dominator alme*),[135] and that all has consistence in Him (*omnia in Ipso constant*).[136]

The monastery, the convent, or the house are created so that those who live there might learn to cry out before everyone, in every instant – their whole life is made for this – that Christ is the only thing that makes the world's existence worthwhile.

So, the dwelling place – that lives as a family, a monastery, a convent, a house of the *Memores Domini*,[137] or as a group of *Fraternity*[138] – is the place, the temple where one learns to see in time and space, and in the other person, the Mystery of Christ. In this way we can understand why the community in a school or in a university is also like a home or a family; or even a community in the workplace, the community in one's neighbourhood, or a particular group is a home or a family, part of the overall, larger family that we call the Church. In this way, we also discover the value of that piece of the Church that exists where we live, called the parish, in other words the reality of God's love nearest to our home (etymologically "parish" means "near home"). There, the community, the friendship we share, is nourished by the sacraments, and by the Word of God that is proclaimed. What a great image the parish is, when we think that it lives as the Church! A parish cannot exist alone. It is a piece of the Church in the place where I live.

In the home, in the family, amongst those friends, we continually meet the Event of that Presence which, when it is acknowledged, changes the way we look at and feel ourselves and all things. In the house, you see the Mystery of Christ present as a face. You learn precisely from the difficulties in the relationships – enlightened by the judgment of His presence – to see the Mystery of Christ in the other person. For each one of us the companionship becomes true as it coalesces in the space of a real daily dwelling place, a home, a dwelling where everything is judged so as to make you sense their common destiny, their common goal. So the relationship with all things becomes an occasion for good in the present that is passing, continually able to recuperate, to provoke happiness, to be a source of joy, of security and of love, whose summit is forgiveness. The Christian tradition has always had this sense of veneration for the earthly dwelling that re-echoes the glory of Christ in the world:

O bright and splendid home
I have always loved your beauty
And the place where my Lord's glory dwells,
He who built you and possesses you.
May my journey sigh for you:
And I say to Him who made you
That he possesses me, too, within you,
Because he made me, too.
...
Jerusalem, God's eternal dwelling,
May my soul never forget you:
After the love for Christ, be you my joy;
The sweet remembrance of your holy name
Raise me up from the sadness of what oppresses me."[139]

It is another world that we have to build, and we are the first witnesses to it, witnesses to that normally impossible unity that becomes experience and makes us capable of forbearance, of patience and mercy towards others, of total sharing, magnanimity in every circumstance. We have been called to begin the building of this new world. The house is the space where the relationship with Christ is imprinted into all our actions, all our gestures, and thus makes us builders of a new reality.

The dwelling (family, monastery, house) indicates the reality in which we live, in our day-to-day relationships, with patience, with understanding, where everything is for us, where everything is welcoming, where everything spurs us to hope, where everything soothes our wounds, where the whole of us, all that we are, is welcomed. As Gregory of Nyssa said, "The bond of our unity is genuine glory."[140]

Through these capillaries the Church lives in the broad context of the whole world. The Church is the reality to which God has entrusted the meaning of time. So the Church carries the meaning of history, year by year, century by century, from man to man. Outside the Church, everything falls to pieces and turns to rubble. So, on the contrary, each one of us is called, as the prophet Isaiah said, to be "re-builder of ruined houses,"[141] of ruined mankind. Each one of us, where he is, day after day, becomes a sign of Jesus' goodness, of His will for man's good: "He turned and saw those who were following him and took pity on them because they were like sheep without a shepherd."[142] We are part of His leadership, His pity for mankind in search of good, of truth, of love, of justice and happiness. For "who could ever speak of Christ's own love for man, overflowing with peace?"[143]

An Event continually generates a bond, a belonging, a new way of life, a new morality, a perfection that bears the fruit that collaborates in the earthly garden, the earthly paradise. Thus we have our part in bringing about God's plan, in the explosion of the human glory of Christ in history.

9 THE PERSUASIVE WAY IN WHICH THE HOLY SPIRIT INTERVENES IN HISTORY — CHARISM

It is the gift of the Holy Spirit that establishes and determines for each of us the concrete dwelling place in the Church, a human companionship that makes the journey to destiny more persuasive.[144] This gift of God's charity makes faith possible, that awareness of the presence of what began as a Fact in history two thousand years ago.

For the Event happens today according to a specific form of time and space that enables us to face it in a certain way and makes it more understandable, more persuasive, and more educationally effective. This characteristic intervention of the Spirit of Christ, which provokes the Event existentially in a time and space, is called a "charism." In order that the Church, made up of men whom Christ has taken hold of and made part of his Body in Baptism, be an operatively effective reality in the world, men have to become aware of what has happened, aware of the encounter that Christ has had with them, and operate on the basis of that awareness.

Cardinal Ratzinger has observed that "the faith is a heartfelt obedience to that form of teaching to which we have been entrusted."[145] In His infinite imagination, in His infinite freedom and mobility, the Spirit of God can bring into being a thousand charisms, a thousand ways for man to partake in Christ.[146] A charism is precisely the mode of time, of space, of character, of temperament, and the psychological, affective, intellectual way with which the Lord becomes event for me, and for others in this same way. This way is communicated from me to others, so that between me and *these* people there is an affinity that is not there with everyone else; a stronger, more specific bond of fraternity. This is how Christ remains present amongst us every day, till the end of the world,[147] within the historical circumstances that the Mystery of the Father establishes, and through which He has us acknowledge and love His presence.[148]

The phenomenon of the Movements in the Church, of all the Movements in the Church, is, as John Paul II observed, the self-awareness that arises in the Church's own sphere.[149] For, just as mankind lives in every home that love animates and beautifies, that the breath of this love warms every day, so the Movements make the Church a living home, alive, warm, full of light and word, of affectivity, of explanation, of answer. These are that unity of companionships created by the charisms, by these gifts given by the Spirit to those He chooses, not because of the persons' value, but to bring about His plan, the plan the Father has for the world, that plan that has a historical name – Jesus Christ.

The Spirit of the Lord chooses temperaments that have characteristics more alive with commitment, emotion, and communication of their own experience to others. So a charism vivifies the Church and is at the service of the whole life of the Church. By its nature, every charism, in virtue of its specific identity, is open to recognize all other charisms. Each of the historical modes with which the Spirit puts men in relationship with the Event of Christ is always a "particular," a particular mode of time and space, of temperament, of character. But it is a particular that renders one capable of the whole. The charism exists as a function of the creation of a complete people; in other words, all-embracing and catholic. As we shall see below, all-embracing and catholic are the ultimate frontiers of the idea of a people.

We could use an image: we could say that the charism is like a window through which you see space in its entirety. The proof of a true charism is that it opens you to everything, it doesn't close you in. So someone would be wrong to say, "We are here to build our Movement, not the Church." We must rather say, "We are here to build the Church according to the thrust the Spirit has given us that we call the Movement, in obedience; in other words, in listening to and adhering to the work of the Spirit of Christ that the Church's authority makes its own."

The question of the charism is crucial, because it is the factor that makes belonging to Christ easier existentially; in other words, it is the evidence of the Event present today, inasmuch as it moves us. In this sense the charism introduces us to dogma as a whole. If the charism is the mode with which the Spirit of Christ makes us perceive His exceptional Presence, then it gives us the power to adhere to it with simplicity and affection. It is living the charism that throws light on the objective content of dogma. If you merely study dogmas abstractly, you don't learn them, and above all they have no existential effect on your life. Dogmas are learned and lived in the encounter with and in following the Church, according to the educationally persuasive and existentially compelling accent of the charism. The charism is therefore the mode with which the Spirit makes the perception of dogma, the perception of the content of the Event as a whole easier, more conscious and fruitful.

In the Church, born of the Spirit of Christ, died and risen, ontologically everything is a charism. The first charism is the Institution, because this is the instrument of the presence of the Spirit of Christ who acts and communicates Himself in the Magisterium and in the Sacraments. But to avoid Magisterium and Sacraments being understood as isolated parts of the unity and the totality of the Christian experience, that is to say reduced to the individualistic measure of the single person, they have to be lived according to the logic and dynamics of communion, which is the very nature of the Church. Then these substantial, institutional charisms are perceived for what they are, through the existentiality of the particular charism, given by the Spirit in function of the overall experience of the Church.

This dynamic is moreover the answer to a temptation particularly widespread in the Church today, according to which the involvement of laypeople in the mission of the Church is perceived as a democratically felt participation in a "power" reductively conceived according to worldly categories.

The question of the relationship between charism and institution therefore appears crucial; this highlights the fact that the two terms are not mutually extrinsic.[150] Every charism regenerates the Church everywhere, it regenerates the institution everywhere, obeying ultimately what guarantees the particular charism itself – Grace, Sacrament, Magisterium. If the particular charism is the terminal through which the Spirit of God is transmitted and through which the acknowledgment of His Event becomes possible today, then the charism of the institution is such because it is the sphere of the life of this terminal. To deny the novelty of a particular charism means to stifle the institution's vitality. On the other hand, the *raison d'être* of a particular charism is justified only in relationship to the whole. John Paul II expresses the nature of the relationship between charism and institution in terms of *co-essentiality*. "In the Church, the institutional aspect and the charismatic aspect ... are co-essential and concur with life, with renewal, with sanctification, albeit in different ways and such that there is a mutual exchange, a mutual communion.[151]

A charism in action: responsibility of each one

"A moving example of this paternity of the Institution, referred to the history of the Movement of Communion and Liberation, is the figure of Pope Paul VI. The first time he called me, when he was still archbishop of Milan, was to offer me some observations. On that occasion he told me, 'I don't understand your ideas and your methods very well, but I see the fruits, and I tell you, go ahead like this.' Years later, in 1975, when seventeen thousand of us went to Rome, he called me to the door of St Peter's at the end of Mass, and the first phrase was, 'Father Giussani, this is the way, go ahead like this.' Exactly the same as the first time."[152]

We have to grow, to mature, and to act in the world according to the particular "form of teaching" with which the Lord has chosen to meet us. We have always to remember the two poles of the relationship that, in the Event created by God, is brought about between us and Him. On one hand, He has us enter into the great people of the mysterious body of Christ, the heir of His chosen people; on the other hand, He touches us according to a determined originality taken up by the Spirit, according to a particular form, according to a particular charism. We experience the whole people of God better, the more we are faithful to our charism, as it were, to our personality imbued by the Spirit, to the personal makeup that God has given us, inasmuch as it is completely taken up in His eternal plan. To draw back from the "form of teaching to which we have been entrusted" is the first step towards tiredness, boredom, confusion, distraction, and even despair.

But in this great companionship in which God has placed us with His Event the best among men are not found. "We are no better than our Fathers," said a song of Father Cocagnac.[153] Even if God is able to raise up children of Abraham from stones,[154] it is not the best amongst men who are part of this companionship; precisely for this reason, what remains clear is the miracle of the Lord's communication that has happened in our life. We are not better than others. St Paul recalled it well in his first letter to the Corinthians, "Consider your own call, brothers. There are not many of you who were wise according to the flesh, not many were powerful, not many of noble birth; but God chose what is foolish in the world to shame the wise. He chose what is weak in the world to shame the strong. God chose what is low and despised in the world to bring to nothing the things that are, so that no human being might boast in God's presence. He is the source of your life in Christ Jesus, whom God made our wisdom, our righteousness and sanctification and redemption; therefore, as it is written, whoever boasts, let him boast of the Lord."[155] Low and despised, that's what we are. But we can boast of the Lord, not of our own merit but His. So let's pay attention to what St James says, "Speak and act like people who must be judged according to the law of freedom, because there will be judgment without mercy for those who have not used mercy themselves; mercy triumphs over judgment."[156]

The essence of the charism of Communion and Liberation can be summed up in the announcement – full of enthusiasm and awe – that God has become man, and that this Man is present in a "sign" of single-heartedness, of communion, of community, of a people in unity. Only in God made man, only in His presence and, therefore, only in some way through the form of His presence, can man be man and mankind be human. This is the source of morality and mission.

Everyone bears responsibility for the charism he has encountered. Everyone is the cause of the decline or increase of the charism, is terrain upon which the charism is wasted or bears fruit. It is a very serious matter for each one to become aware of this responsibility, as urgency, as loyalty and faithfulness. To obscure or diminish this responsibility means to obscure and diminish the intensity of the effect that the history of our charism has on the Church of God and on society.

Each person gives a personal identification, a personal version of the charism to which we have been called and to which we belong. Inevitably the more one becomes responsible, the more the charism passes through one's temperament, through that vocation irreducible to any other, that is, one's person. The person of each one of us has its concreteness, its own mentality, its own temperament, its own life circumstances, and above all its own movement of freedom.

So the charism takes up diverse and approximate inflections according to each one's generosity. The approximation is measured by one's generosity, where capacity, temperament, personal taste, etc., are combined (one could do what one likes with the charism and its history; reduce it, paralyze it, stress certain aspects at the expense of others, bend it to one's own taste and advantage, or even abandon it out of negligence, or obstinacy, or superficiality).

The charism rises or falls according to each one's generosity. This is the law of generosity, to give your life for the work of an Other. Everyone, in his every action, every one of his days, in all his imaginings, in all his resolutions, in everything he does, must be concerned with comparing his criteria with the charism, just as it emerged at the origins of our common history. Comparison with the charism, just as we have received it, tends to correct the singularity of the version, of the translation; it is continuous correction and reawakening. Methodologically, morally, and pedagogically this comparison must therefore be our greatest concern.[157] Otherwise the charism becomes a pretext and a cue for what we want; it covers up and justifies what we want. To limit this temptation common to everyone, we must make it our normal behaviour to compare ourselves with the charism as correction and as a continually re-awakened ideal. This comparison must become a habit, a virtue. This is our virtue: the comparison with the charism in its originality through the fleeting things that God uses. Here again we meet the importance of the ephemeral. For now, the comparison is with the person with whom everything began. This person can be dissolved, but the texts left behind and the uninterrupted succession – if God wills – of the people indicated as the reference point, as true interpretation of what happened, become the instrument for correction and for reawakening; they become the instrument for morality. The line of references indicated is the most living thing in the present, because a text alone can be interpreted wrongly. It is difficult to interpret it wrongly, but it can happen.

Giving one's life for the work of an Other always implies a link between the word "Other" and something historical, concrete, tangible, describable, photographable, with a name and a surname. Without this historical factor our pride imposes itself. This is certainly ephemeral, but in the worst sense of the word.

Giving one's life for the work of an Other, not abstractly, is to say something that has a precise historical reference. For us it means that all that we do, our whole life, is for the increase of the charism we have been given to participate in, which has its chronology and a face that can be described; it indicates names and surnames and, at the origin, has one name and one surname.

If giving one's life for the work of an Other does not have a precise reference point, then its historicity fades away, its concreteness is lost; you no longer give your life for the work of an Other, but for your own interpretation of it, for your own personal taste, for your own profit or for your own point of view. To speak of a charism without historicity is not to speak of a Catholic charism.

3

A New People in History
for the Human Glory of Christ

I   A NEW PROTAGONIST IN HISTORY

The companionship of those whom Christ has assimilated to Himself in the Church, His Body, lives and reveals itself as a new people, the People of God. First, let us see what the characteristics of a people are, and then how this particular people, the People of God, are revealed in the history of mankind.

The existence of a people requires a bond between persons created by an event that is perceived as decisive for its historical meaning, for their destiny, and for that of the world. An event gives rise to a people by pointing out a stable bond of belonging between persons who were unrelated up to that moment, just as the event of a child completes the beginning of a family. Let us take an example. Imagine two families living in houses built on piles in the middle of a river that periodically swells. The unity between these two families, then five, then ten as generations pass, is a continuous fight for survival, and ultimately for affirming life. The bond that grew between them makes them seek a greater and greater consistency of their life as it was started. The reality that is born is judged to be positive, a good, and this also implies a defence, with all the ingenuity and the operative energy needed, against whoever attacks it. A yeast among them keeps them united, supports their life – it is the dawn of a people.

The life of a people is determined by a common ideal, by a value that makes it worthwhile living, struggling, suffering and even dying for, a common ideal that makes everything worthwhile. It is a dynamic that St Augustine already sensed when he observed in *City of God* that "a people is the joining together of rational beings associated in the agreed communion of the things it loves," and he adds that to know the nature of each people one needs to look at what it loves ("ut videatur qualis quisque populus sit, illa sunt intuenda quae diligit").[1] Second, the life of a people is determined by the identification of the suitable instruments and the methods for attaining the acknowledged ideal, for tackling the needs and challenges that gradually arise from the historical circumstances. Third, it is determined by the mutual fidelity in which one helps the other on the journey towards the realization of the ideal. A people exists where there is the memory of a common history that is accepted as a historic task to be carried out.

So the acknowledgment of the ideal gives rise to a powerful commitment to work, which strives to create the tools needed as best it can. This expresses itself ultimately in the people's charity, which has each one carry the other's weight. In this sense, the "we" enters into the definition of the self. It is the people that defines the self's destiny, its operative capacity and affective (and therefore fertile and creative) genius. If the people's "we" enters into the definition of the "I," then the "I" reaches its greatest maturity, as acknowledgment of its personal destiny and as its overall affectivity, identifying itself with the life and ideal of the people. Therefore, without friendship, that is to say, without gratuitous mutual affirmation of a common destiny, there is no people.

The most mysterious thing is that the successful formation of a people inevitably implies the prospect that its own good will be good for the world and for everyone else. This emerges clearly when the people acquire a certain security and dignity, and their ideal matures and is affirmed. This is the origin of every civilization, just as its disappearance marks its decline; a civilization declines when it is no longer able to live up to the ideal that generated it.

In this sense, the Hebrew people can be the symbol of all peoples. The people of Israel was born of an event in history,[2] born of the promise made to Abraham that his descendants would be more numerous than the stars in the sky and the sand on the sea-shore.[3] Thus a covenant was established between Yahweh, who will be their God, and the Israelites, who will be his people.

In a mysterious continuity with this history,[4] a new People is born from Christ, a People that shows itself on the streets of Jerusalem and under Solomon's portico.[5] The idea of belonging, of being God's property, which defined the Hebrew people's self-awareness, is once again found as the content of the awareness of the first Christians. For from its birth, the group conceived of itself as the unity of those who belonged to Christ and were carrying on His mission. James, who was the first head of the Jerusalem community, says in one of his speeches, quoting the prophet Amos, "Brothers, listen to me. Simon has stated how from the beginning God wanted to choose amongst the pagans a people so as to consecrate them to his name. The words of the prophets agree on this as it is written, 'After these things, I will come back and rebuild the tent of David that was fallen; I will repair its ruins and raise it up so that all other men may search for the LORD and all the peoples over which my name has been invoked, says the LORD who does these things which are known to Him from all eternity.'"[6]

However, belonging to the Church brings a crucial novelty – the Christians are the People of God, but the criterion of belonging to this people is no longer based on ethnic origin or sociological unity. The new People is made up of those whom God has chosen and brought together in the acceptance of his Son, died and risen.[7]

As we saw in the preceding chapter, the generative and dynamic law of this People is election. The elect, those whom Christ has called, receive the mission entrusted to them as a task so as to carry out the Father's plan in the world. Being sent is inherent in being chosen through the fact of Baptism. A disciple of Christ, a baptized person, cannot be conceived of unless for the mission.

One is born and baptized for the mission; the grace of the encounter and the education of belonging are given for the mission. And if someone does not reach the age of freedom and mature awareness, then we have to echo what Péguy said about the Holy Innocents: their greatness and their holiness are resolved in the fact that they were made, without knowing it and without having done anything, part of the Mystery of Christ's mission, which is the salvation of the world.[8]

There is a page of the Gospel that existentially documents the new People bursting into history, with the new task of belonging to Christ and of taking part in His mission.[9]

From Peter's "yes" a new people is born: "Feed my flock"

Peter's *yes* to Christ opens a connection between a person's vocation and God's universal plan. What is this connection between the personal moment and the mysterious whole of God's plan, and what does it produce? In answer to Peter's *yes*, Jesus expresses this connection with a phrase that is easy to understand: "Feed my sheep. Feed my lambs. Feed my flock."[10] It is as if Jesus were to have said, "Lead my flock, I will lead my flock through you, the Rock on which my building in the world, my plan for the world, stands and will develop."[11] Peter's belonging to Christ thus becomes a participation in God's universal plan. "Feed my sheep": lead this new living group that becomes the protagonist of history, the instrument of the victory and of the human glory of Christ in history.

Peter's *yes* is the beginning of a new relationship of the individual person with the whole of reality. It is the beginning of a new relationship, not only between each person and Jesus but with the whole of reality. The relationship between man and woman, and between parents and children, changes shape, the rules of education change shape. The way of looking at heaven and earth, of getting up in the morning and going to bed at night is different, and so is the way you go to work, the way you deal with things that don't work out, with a doubt that disturbs you, with questions that weigh on your heart. There is a change in your attitude to death and to birth.

At the root of this change of attitudes is the triumph of the pity that Christ had on man. "He turned and saw all the people following Him and He had pity on them because they were like sheep without a shepherd."[12] Peter was the first shepherd that He placed to lead His flock, in order that, in the various ups and downs in the relationship between men and reality what is seen to triumph should be Christ's pity for man. Peter, guarantee of the unity of this new People in history, ensures the permanence of the newness that Christ introduced into the world so as to sustain man's hope.

Through forgiveness and untiring activity

In the first place, Peter's *yes* to Christ produces a new reality through forgiveness. As Jesus asks, "Simon, do you love me?" He destroys all resentment, all remembrance of the betrayals of that poor man before Him. If Peter's *yes* is to produce a new humanity, a new people, a new current of humanity, one that is different, alert, vigilant, with a mentality and a gaze that sees, judges, and deals with things differently from the world, if this *yes* is to become evident in its fecundity, decisive for the history of mankind and protagonist of human events, then it must arise from, stand upon, and build upon forgiveness, accepting it. Accepting forgiveness is perhaps what is most difficult, even though it is very simple.

Peter's *yes* creates a new people on forgiveness. It is pronounced out of the awareness that that face that asks him, "Simon, do you love me?" is full of forgiveness. Peter's *yes* is built on this forgiveness and obtains this forgiveness for everyone. This is why the Abbot tells Miguel Mañara that all that he might have done in the past is as if reduced to nothing.[13] It takes an infinite power to reduce something that is to nothing. Forgiveness is first a reduction to nothing of all the evil I have done, but even of all the evil I will do, because a month from now, a year from now, formally I should have to say the same as today. A true mother or father knows something of what this almighty power means when they cancel the record of the wrongs, great and small, done by their children. The comparison is blurred by our smallness and weakness, but it is the only comparison possible. A father and mother forgive their children continually; they must go on forgiving them if the children are to grow. And there will be no end to this forgiveness, it must rather increase with the passing of time.

Second, Peter's *yes* unleashes an activity that is in contradiction with the approximations and denials of worldly hatred. "Whoever has this hope in Him, purifies himself as He is pure."[14] He is not purified all at once, he does not reach holiness straightaway, but his whole life is a purification: "purifies himself as He is pure." So he makes a habit of reciting the Angelus as he gets up in the morning, offering his day with the awareness that his own weakness, in the mistakes he will make that day, is already forgiven: "I offer You this day, my God, however it goes, so that You can forgive it, cancelling the memory of my evil, so that You keep it tending, striving towards You," like St Peter and St John running to see the tomb[15] from which Jesus had risen.

The new People is born from this forgiveness and from this untiring activity, activity not paid for by what it builds (because it succeeds). Here there is no measuring, no success, no failure. In forgiveness, standing upon forgiveness, you start over and over again, a thousand times a day.

The People of God, one and manifold, affects history

The people of God that is born is *one*. "You who have been baptized have become one with Christ ... you are one (*eis*) in Christ Jesus."[16] Peter's *yes* to Christ brings with it the beginning of a new world that is documented visibly in the unity amongst those who acknowledge Him. It is documented phenomenally as a unity that has an original, ontological depth. It is an organism in the real sense of the word: it is the mysterious Body of Christ. There is another word used for this ontology, *communio*, communion of being, for which "you are all one (*eis*) in Christ Jesus." The Christ Event goes on in history, it is present in every "present," documenting itself phenomenally as a unity of men who are together because of Him, because they have acknowledged being chosen by Him.

This unity is not a homogenization, a group of meaningless faces; it is made up of precise faces. The unity of the People is not a homogenization, it is rich in nuances because every reality that constitutes it is born of a history in which an "encounter" placed people together and marked out their road. From the moment of the encounter, the journey towards purity becomes easier to understand, to follow, and to love, and more fruitful. Every part of this People is born of a particular grace of the Spirit that is called a charism.

The unity of people who acknowledge Him in a particular environment, because they are linked with the communion of all those who believe in Christ present, has its effect on society, as the present, and on history, as the continuity of society. This unity makes the baptized person the new protagonist who, out of love for Christ, strives to create a more human world for everyone in His Name. Because of its very nature, this unity (whether it be of two or of two hundred million) has an effect on society, even as regards politics, and on history as culture and civilization. In this sense, the Gospel contains the clear and complete formula of the method for evangelization, "That they be one, so that the world may believe that You sent me."[17]

Cardinal Newman wrote of this visible and unceasing current of humanity in history,

"Strictly speaking, the Christian Church, as being a visible society, is necessarily a political power or party. It may be a party triumphant, or a party under persecution; but a party it always must be, prior in existence to the civil institutions with which it is surrounded, and from its latent divinity formidable and influential, even to the end of time. The grant of permanency was made in the beginning, not to the mere doctrine of the Gospel, but to the Association itself built upon the doctrine; in prediction, not only of the indestructibility of Christianity, but of the medium also through which it was to be manifested to the world. Thus the Ecclesiastical Body is a divinely appointed means towards realizing the great evangelical blessings."[18]

Defence of the life of the people and mutual help

Tenderness for Christ[19] makes us become new protagonists in society, even in politics and in history, to the extent of creating a new civilization. This is the most sensational consequence that sprang from the invisible nucleus that the Holy Spirit created in the womb of a young woman, and then developed to take on the dimensions of a people.

Christians are men who, in acknowledging themselves in companionship, in friendship, live a struggle, striving with their whole selves towards the aim of life as the common ideal of the people. For these times, in which, as T.S. Eliot says, "men have forgotten all gods, except Usury, Lust and Power,"[20] these gods count less than the striving for the ideal. Christians live therefore without being scandalized by their own mistakes, or by betrayal – the most painful drawback of incoherence – but continuously recovering the horizon of the ideal. Life is conceived as striving towards Destiny, as a struggle for the good, thus it becomes easy to join together to help each other.

The Event that suddenly unites those who meet it and accept it, expresses its unifying principle first as the realization of subsidiarity. Each one helps the other and tries to make up for what the other lacks. It is a concrete subsidiarity, a daily one if possible, which makes life easier and provides defence against the enemy that threatens the life of the people. This enemy is the "world," in other words, human reality when conceived programmatically as opposing all reference to Christ.[21]

The awareness of being chosen to participate in the building of the Kingdom of God unleashes a new wave into our hearts, which – through that narrow path that is called the cross, sacrifice – makes loving feeling become genuine mutual charity. To live this is to work together for peace and therefore for conscientiousness, for the support of life, for the perception of life as full of meaning, as we await the fulfillment of its final meaning.

In achieving these aims, the meaning of the people is fulfilled. It is fulfilled in view of eternity; in other words, to live the eternal within one's normal activity. In this way, the people collaborate in the aim of creation, collaborate with Jesus on the Cross, experiencing the gradual intensification of the final light, love and joy, in which Christ's Resurrection, as the fulfillment of the Cross, penetrates and assimilates all that we know, use, and live together.

The new People that Christ has generated in the world, this irresistible torrent – despite the tragic events that it must pass through
– is made of people who in some way accept living these things.
Whenever they don't understand, they ask God for the grace to
understand, and ask their brothers for the grace of assistance.

The Christians' responsibility is that of being what they have
known, what has become part of their mind and heart. So we
are responsible for being what we are, what we have been called
to by Jesus in Baptism and in the encounter that made it blossom. Our responsibility is that of being friends according to the
encounter we have had.[22] And this friendship cannot fail to have
its effect on the relationships that are formed in the family, at
work, and in social and political life. So we see the present-day
relevance of what Alasdair MacIntyre said of the situation in
Europe in the late Roman Empire:

"A crucial turning point in that earlier history occurred when
men and women of good will turned aside from the task of shor-
ing up the Roman imperium and ceased to identify the continua-
tion of civility and moral community with the maintenance of
that imperium. What they set themselves to achieve instead –
often not recognizing fully what they were doing – was the construction of new forms of community within which the moral
life could be sustained so that both morality and civility might
survive the coming ages of barbarism and darkness."[23]

The friendship of those called by Jesus in Baptism is the beginning of the community MacIntyre speaks of, the beginning
of a new culture, of a new understanding of society and State,
and of the world. In this way new human communities were
born, which, to use the words of John Paul II, are the only possible means for overcoming the desolation of much of modern
society: "The re-awakening of the Christian people to a greater
awareness of the Church, building living communities in which
the following of Christ becomes concrete, affects the relationships of which the day is made and embraces the dimensions
of life: this is the only adequate answer to the secularising culture that threatens Christian principles and the moral values of
society." This threat mainly affects two things. First, the pledge

of human happiness, which the bible calls "heritage," and the certain expectation of this constitutes and defines the true man; second, the existence of the people. The aim of power seems to be the elimination of the people, as the unity of men who have a common ideal and who identify the means for reaching it, in particular, the Christian people, which pursues its true destiny in the companionship generated by Christ.

2 FOR THE HUMAN GLORY OF CHRIST

The glory of Jesus, as the aim of the Mystery of the Father, of the Father's plan, as the aim of all that is, belongs to this world, to time and space; in other words, to history. The human glory of Christ is the realization of what He is in the Father's plan within the terms of time and space, the coming about of the power He has been given by the Father, to whom He said, "You have given me authority over all flesh."[24] This "realization" becomes the fascination and the impressiveness of the Presence of God in our life, it becomes the You whom we are to obey, the mercy we are to implore. This is what gives certainty to life, as for a child in its mother's and father's arms: even in a storm he is not afraid.[25] If I find myself out of my depth, I am sure that in this disproportion Christ will make His glory seen. It is through the joyful fulfillment of my presence in the world that my collaboration in His glory is realized. In the past, spiritual directors used to tell young people, "If you do not offer this hour of study for Jesus, His glory is reduced in the world." The glory of Jesus in history is less if I do not offer my time. The glory of Jesus is a fact of this world, not of the next world. In the next world, "God will be all in all,"[26] there will no longer be exceptions or obscurity. But not in this world. The altar destroyed, to recall the image used by the great poet Eliot in *Choruses from "The Rock,"* remains as an imposing truth:

The Church must be forever building, for it is forever
   decaying within and attacked from without;
For this is the law of life; and you must remember that while
   there is time of prosperity

The people will neglect the Temple, and in time of adversity
  they will decry it.
What life have you if you have not life together? There is no
  life that is not in community,
And no community not lived in praise of God.
Even the anchorite who meditates alone,
For whom the days and nights repeat the praise of God,
Prays for the Church, the Body of Christ incarnate.
And now you live dispersed on ribbon roads,
And no man knows or cares who is his neighbour
Unless his neighbour makes too much disturbance,
But all dash to and fro in motor cars,
Familiar with the roads and settled nowhere.
Nor does the family even move about together,
But every son would have his motor cycle,
And daughters ride away on casual pillions.
Much to cast down, much to build, much to restore;
Let the work not delay, time and the arm not waste;
Let the clay be dug from the pit, let the saw cut the stone,
Let the fire not be quenched in the forge.[27]
And if the Temple is to be cast down
We must first build the Temple.[28]

We fight for the glory of Christ in time, in history. We too are "sent"
for this battle. We are promised victory,[29] but it will be on the last
day, the day in which the resurrection is complete, the day of which
Jesus said, "As for that day and that hour, nobody knows, not even
the angels of heaven, nor even the Son, but only the Father."[30]

Our passion is for the human glory of Christ, not simply
"Christ," which could end up just being a name, or even be
blurred according to our imagination or our expectations, and
in the end reduced. For the mortal danger in the Church today
is abstractness (even in saying "Christ"); and you can build all
the discourses you want on an abstract word. What overcomes
abstractness is only the present. The present is the real object of
knowledge. All that is not, in some way, in the tangible present
does not exist. Even God, in His existence, must be present here,

since presence is the characteristic of God's being. As St Thomas says, "The name 'He who is' means being in the present, and this corresponds in the most absolute way to God himself, whose being knows neither past nor future."[31]

What is present amongst us is Christ the incarnate Word, born of woman, died and risen. A man of two thousand years ago cannot be present here; if He is present here then He is God. This is the glorification of Christ. I acknowledge a Presence that is dominant, crucial. If it were not so, then it would not be present. We need to help each other to rediscover reality, to rediscover what is, to help each other look, touch, see, and feel everything that is, so as to come to be able to say, "Only He is." This is the human glory of Christ: His being, here and now, the exhaustive meaning of everything, becoming tangible and possible to experience. If something were to remain outside Christ, He would be nothing, because He would not be its Lord.

Apart from the passion for the human glory of Christ, nothing can give joy to the heart with the slightest stability and balance, and this joy becomes the witness to His glory. "People of Sion, see, your Lord is coming to save all the peoples; the Lord will show His glory and your heart will rejoice."[32] When Jesus said, "I have told you all these things so that my joy may be in you and your joy be complete,"[33] He was referring to the mystery of the history that has His glory as its aim. St Paul says the same thing, though he seems to be saying the opposite, "When I came to you brothers, I did not come proclaiming to you the testimony of God in lofty words or wisdom. For I decided to know nothing among you except Jesus Christ and Him crucified."[34] With these words St Paul stresses that "complete joy" does not coincide with the realization of a plan for world domination, according to man-made analyses or values. The fact that this cannot be foreseen means that we are promised not the historical outcome of Christ's domination of the world, but only being ready for "that" day in which Christ will place the content of His final victory into the Father's hands: "And when all things are subjected to Him, then the Son himself will also be subjected to Him who put all things under Him, that God may be all in all."[35]

Forty years in this fight

Those more faithful among us know very well that for forty years this has been our desire, our daily programme, and our entreaty to God every day, especially in the *Angelus*; a daily effort – ascesis – taken on continually in the awareness of our own limitations and of a suffering that is part of Christ's Cross: "My suffering is part of Your Cross, O Christ."[36] What greater nobility could we have inherited, what greater grace? As Eliot says:

> Without the meaning there is no time, and that moment of
>   time gave the meaning.
> Then it seemed as if men must proceed from light to light, in
>   the light of the Word,
> Through the Passion and Sacrifice saved in spite of their
>   negative being;
> Bestial as always before, carnal, self-seeking as always before,
>   selfish and purblind as ever before,
> Yet always struggling, always reaffirming, always resuming
>   their march on the way that was lit by the light;
> Often halting, loitering, straying, delaying, returning, yet
>   following no other way.[37]

Following no other way, for forty years! Always struggling, in the clearer and clearer awareness, every day, of our own weakness, of our own human limitation. "Struggle" is our word. This is the conception of life, of life as morality: struggle or ascesis, as our fathers used to say; a true ascesis, a tension to become better. Life as ascesis, as drama, as striving for the good, is brought into the world only by Christ. All other conceptions are more or less deterministic. For them, the outcome of time is mechanical, not a striving of the intelligence that enlightens the effort of the will.

We recalled the fortieth anniversary of the beginning of our Movement with this phrase: "As we go on maturing, we are a spectacle for ourselves, and, God willing, for others, too. A spectacle, in other words, of limitation and betrayal, and therefore of humiliation, and at the same time of inexhaustible certainty in the power of grace that is given us and is renewed every morning. This gives us the naïve boldness that characterizes us, for which every day of our life is conceived as an offering to God, so that the Church may exist in our bodies and souls through the materiality of our existence." These words express our whole judgment on life and on the world, which would be nothing if the Church were not true as the affirmation of happiness, as the destiny of every man who comes into this world, in day-to-day relationships. There is no separation between the materiality of existence and Christ who is with us, and who holds us in His embrace.

We are well aware of our human frailty, which we share with all men, but we are also aware of the certainty in Christ, which makes us different from all men. So we are also aware of the gladness and optimism that explain the inexorable repetition of our efforts, always struggling.

3 A PEOPLE CONTINUALLY DESTROYED AND REBUILT

From the beginning of the world until the end, the People has an enemy: Satan, in other words, falsehood and discord. As St James says, "For where jealousy and selfish ambition exist, there will be disorder and every vile practice ... What causes wars, and what causes fightings among you? Is it not your passions that are at war in your members? You desire and do not have; so you kill. And you covet and cannot obtain; so you fight and wage war. You do not have, because you do not ask. You ask and do not receive, because you ask wrongly, to spend it on your passions. Unfaithful creatures! Do you not know that friendship with the world is enmity with God?"[38]

The world's hatred for Christ

If Christ is a present Event, we meet Him every day. Yet we do not realize it because we are distracted. We meet Him every day. He crosses our path and calls us friends. But alongside a kind of moved acknowledgment and a vague emotion that most people feel when they hear the name Jesus Christ, there is a hostility towards Him today that there has never been before, except in the earliest days, when they crucified Him and killed His martyrs, when they outlawed His witnesses in the first centuries. It is a generalized hostility, fed and produced systematically, so well supported theoretically that we get accustomed to it day by day without realizing it, and this reveals how distracted we are. And when we do realize it – and this is worse – we pretend not to hear and not to see; we don't consider it important.

> But it seems that something has happened that has never happened before: though we know not just when, or why, or how, or where.
> Men have left GOD not for other gods, they say, but for no god; and this has never happened before
> That men both deny gods and worship gods, professing first Reason,
> And then Money, and Power, and what they call Life, or Race, or Dialectic.
> The Church disowned, the tower overthrown, the bells upturned, what have we to do
> But stand with empty hands and palms turned upwards
> In an age which advances progressively backwards?[39]

With his sensitivity as a poet and a man of great faith, Péguy observed, "For the first time, for the first time after Jesus, we have seen, before our eyes, we are about to see before our eyes a new world arising, if not a city; a new society forming, if not a city – modern society, the modern world. A world, a society in formation, or at least, assembling, growing, after Jesus, without Jesus. And the most terrible thing, my friends, we mustn't deny it, is that they have managed. What gives a capital importance to our generation and to the time we live in, my friends, is what puts you at a unique watershed in the history of the world, is what puts you in a tragic, unique situation. You are the first. You are the first of the modern men, you are the first before whom, before whose eyes has happened, and you have caused to happen, this singular work, this foundation of the modern world, this establishment of the intellectual party of the modern world"[40]

For the first time since Jesus came the world is no longer Christian. The man who ran to Jesus's enemies to accuse him when Lazarus was raised from the tomb,[41] this man has managed to create a world and a society without Christ. He has managed with our connivance, with our collaboration. The awful problem is that ours is a world – a society – without Christ; the family, school, work, life and social initiatives, government, war and peace, without Christ.

With enigmatic words, on Wednesday, 23 July 1975, Pope Paul VI said in a famous address, "Where is the 'People of God,' of which so much has been said, and is still being said, where is it? This ethnic entity *sui generis*, distinguished and qualified by its religious and messianic, priestly and prophetic character, if you will, that converges all towards Christ, as its focus, and that derives all from Christ? What is its form? How is it characterized? How is it organized? How does it carry out its ideal, invigorating mission, in the society wherein it is immersed? We know very well that the People of God, has now, historically, a name more familiar to everyone: it is the Church, the Church loved, to the shedding of blood, by Christ, His Mystical Body, His work in the course of perennial construction; our Church, One, Holy, Catholic and Apostolic; but who truly knows it and lives it? Who has that *sensus ecclesiae*, that is to say, the awareness of belonging to a special, a supernatural society, that is a living body with Christ its head, and forms with Him that *totus Christus*, mankind's unitary communion in Christ, which constitutes the great plan of God's love for us, and on which depends our salvation?"[42]

He repeated this judgment more urgently some years later: "There is a great unrest in this moment in the world and in the Church, and what is in question is the faith. These days I find myself repeating that obscure phrase of Jesus in St Luke's Gospel: 'When the Son of man returns, will He still find faith on earth?' Books are published in which the faith is in retreat on important points, that Episcopates keep quiet and don't find these books strange. This seems strange to me. I sometimes read the Gospel on the end of time and I realize that some signs of that end are emerging in this moment. Are we near the end? This we will never know. We have to be always prepared, but it may all still go on for a very long time. What strikes me, when I consider the Catholic world, is that within Catholicism there seems at times to predominate a non-Catholic line of thought, and it could happen tomorrow that this non-Catholic thought becomes the strongest. But this will never represent the thought of the Church. A little flock must survive, however small it may be."[43]

The refrain of one of Tomás Luis de Victoria's most beautiful Responsories for Holy Week says, "Consilium fecerunt inimici mei / adversum me, dicentes: / Venite, mittamus lignum in panem eius, / et eradamus eum de terra viventium" (My enemies took counsel against me saying, 'Come let us put poison in his bread, so as to remove him from the land of the living').[44] This is the definition of the hatred of the society that does not accept Him, that does not agree with Him, or acknowledge Him, a society that is hostile towards Him.

To speak of hatred for Christ is no exaggeration. It is one of the most painful themes that Jesus took up in His last discourse before He died.[45] This hatred characterizes human history. It is, as it were, the on-going result of the mysterious wound of original sin in human history. It articulates and becomes concrete day by day, through all the powers, as an enormously evil and mendacious possibility. For it is power that takes up and personifies this possibility, gives it life, intelligence, and weapons, and makes a wicked plan of it. It is in this hatred that the father of lies works, making use of all the powers, that father of lies described by Jesus when he speaks of Satan to the Pharisees.[46] Hatred for Jesus is the theme necessary for every power that does not consciously draw its humble and dramatic origin from obedience to the supreme power of the Father who makes all things,[47] from obedience to the destiny of victory and glory which is the destiny of the man Christ, the justice of God, the name that gives the meaning of the plan of the universe and of history.

It is not pessimism that makes us say these things. But if Jesus said, "as the world hated me, so it will hate you,"[48] not only are we responsible for the hatred for Christ, but, since we are His people, we, too, are victims of the world's hatred (as when some people fail to get a place in university or in schools, or others are not accepted for a job because they are Catholics).

The last capillary of this hatred for Christ is our self, forgetful and indifferent. The most relevant, most decisive end point, is in me, in us, in our mind and heart. The refusal begins there, forgetfulness is generated and cultivated there, absence and inhospitality harden there – in us, in me. It is a hatred we do not necessarily express outwardly, but we clearly live more and more estranged from Him. Even a very Christian family can live in an unchristian way from morning till night. You don't need to kill or to break all of the Ten Commandments at once to be unchristian. What makes us unchristian is the absence of Christ. The absence of Christ is the absence of His life. This tends to produce an indifference to reality that becomes lack of responsibility for your own personal and collective existence. It becomes amorality. The outcome of this is to give in to whomever shouts loudest, to whomever has most power. But this indifference to reality originates in indifference to the experience of faith, because it is through this that God stirs the soul and calls us to responsibility. Thus life is lost in the confusion in which everything becomes licit and in which everything becomes hostile. Suffering is increased and we are consumed by rebellion or cynicism instead of being stirred to collaboration for rebuilding a people.

A people rebuilt

In this state of affairs, which would be the norm without God's intervention, the initiative of Christ present continually makes His people live and renews it. God created in history a people whose experience is a prophecy of this. The people of Israel came back from exile to re-establish itself, against all human expectation. Ezra the priest and Nehemiah the governor gathered the people together, once they had finally rebuilt the walls of Jerusalem, to proclaim the law of Moses; in other words, the rule of life. Let us read the moving page of the book of Nehemiah that immortalized this event.

And all the people gathered as one man into the square before the Water Gate; and they told Ezra the scribe to bring the book of the law of Moses which the LORD had given to Israel. And Ezra the priest brought the law before the assembly, both men and women and all who could hear with understanding, on the first day of the seventh month. And he read from it facing the square before the Water Gate from early morning until midday, in the presence of the men and the women and those who could understand; and the ears of all the people were attentive to the book of the law. And Ezra the scribe stood on a wooden pulpit which they had made for the purpose; and beside him stood Mattithi'ah, Shema, Anai'ah, Uri'ah, Hilki'ah, and Maasei'ah on his right hand; and Pedai'ah, Mish'a-el, Malchi'jah, Hashum, Hash-bad'danah, Zechari'ah, and Meshul'lam on his left hand. And Ezra opened the book in the sight of all the people, for he was above all the people; and when he opened it all the people stood. And Ezra blessed the LORD, the great God; and all the people answered, "Amen, Amen," lifting up their hands; and they bowed their heads and worshipped the LORD with their faces to the ground. Also Jesh'ua, Bani, Sherebi'ah, Jamin, Akkub, Shab'bethai, Hodi'ah, Ma-asei'ah, Keli'ta, Azari'ah, Jo'zabad, Hanan, Pelai'ah, the Levites, helped the people to understand the law, while the people remained in their places. And they read from the book, from the law of God, clearly; and they gave the sense, so that the people understood the reading. And Nehemi'ah, who was the governor, and Ezra the priest and scribe, and the Levites who taught the people said to all the people, "This day is holy to the LORD your God; do not mourn or weep." For all the people wept when they heard the words of the law. Then he said to them, "Go your way, eat the fat and drink sweet wine and send portions to him for whom nothing is prepared; for this day is holy to our Lord; and do not be grieved, for the joy of the LORD is your strength." So the Levites stilled all the people, saying, "Be quiet, for this day is holy; do not be grieved."[49]

This people, broken down, destroyed, in exile, is made to return "beyond all expectation," not because they had planned it. None of them could have pressed their hope so far, it was beyond their imagination. And yet they returned, they are there in Jerusalem, all reduced to ruins; they rebuild it, stone by stone, and they re-build themselves as a people. So this biblical passage is perhaps the most interesting point in the history of the people of Israel before Christ.

The prophetic presence of this people was fulfilled definitively in Christ and continues unfailingly in the mystery of the Church. For it is the Church that is the great subject of the ongoing human epic for the creation of what John Paul II called "the civilization of truth and love."[50] The subject of this epic is the Christian people, who, born of Baptism, lives on the daily com-panionship in faith, hope, and charity, drawing from the sacra-ments the strength of the risen Christ.[51]

Because of the love we have for the Christian people, the sub-ject of the great human epic, we have always loved its history and we feel like blood-relatives above all to those who, by living their faith in the world, have contributed to creating something new, an objectively recordable newness in history. This explains our cultural preference for the great Benedictine movement that created mediaeval civilization. On this movement of new hu-manity born of Benedictine monasticism, the English historian, Christopher Dawson, wrote:

It was the disciplined and tireless labour of the monks which turned the tide of barbarism in Western Europe and brought back into cultivation the lands which had been deserted and depopulated in the age of the invasions. As Newman writes in a well-known passage on the Mission of St Benedict: "St Benedict found the world, physical and social, in ruins, and his mission was to restore it in the way not of science, but of nature, not as if setting about to do it, not professing to do it in any set time, or by any rare specific, or by any ser-ies of strokes, but so quietly, patiently, gradually, that often till the work was done, it was not known to be doing. It was a restoration rather than a visitation, correction or conver-sion. The new work which he helped to create was a growth rather than a structure. Silent men were observed about the

country, or discovered in the forest, digging, clearing and
building; and other silent men, not seen, were sitting in a
cold cloister, tiring their eyes and keeping their attention
on the stretch, while they painfully copied and recopied the
manuscripts which they had saved. There was no one who
contended or cried out, or drew attention to what was going
on, but by degrees the woody swamp became a hermitage, a
religious house, a farm, an abbey, a village, a seminary,
a school of learning and a city."[52]

4 MISSION AND ECUMENISM: THE NEW CULTURE

The new People, made up of those chosen in Baptism, shares, as
we have said, in Christ's mission, so that God's Kingdom may
come and His will be done. Belonging to Christ's mission as a
new nature changes the self-awareness of our person in such a
way that the principle of action is no longer the "I" but a "You."
To live for an Other indicates the genesis of a new culture: living
no longer for oneself, but for Him who died and rose for us.[53]
This new awareness judges all the relationships of life and makes
us able to love every bit of truth left in anyone, with a positivity
and a critique unknown to the world.

We too are "sent" by the Father

We Christians, too, are called to be, like Jesus, those sent by the
Father. "As the Father sent me, so I am sending you."[54] We have
formed a clearer idea of the mysterious origin of this task, since
no one can say as we do: "Abba, Father."[55] And the aim, the end,
of this overall plan has become clearer, too – the glory of Christ
in the world. "Thy Kingdom come, Thy will be done."[56] His
Kingdom is the glory of Christ in the world, for which "the hour
has come; glorify your Son, so that the Son may glorify you."[57]

But even more profound, more enigmatic, and at the same time
more attractive for us is the heart of the Mystery as the definition
of our person. Not only is the Mystery the origin and the final

aim; it is at work in the ontology, in the supporting structures, in the directives and the criteria for action of our person. So what is our person in this Mystery? What is the meaning of this Mystery of belonging to Christ's mission in which the Father has us share so as to fulfill his aim? How does sharing in this mission determine my life? How do I live the bond with what is, instant by instant, with my new origin?

If we speak of a new origin it is because this is not our origin as creatures, but the origin of the new self in Baptism, which makes it share in the person and mission of Christ. So what produces this passion for the glory of Christ as the aim of every breath?[58] How does this vigilance take shape today? Since we have been taken hold of in Baptism, we are something other than we were and felt before; we are a new creature, which comes from the Father and is for the human glory of the Son.[59]

Overwhelmed by the memory of Christ's love

St Paul wrote to the Christians of Corinth, "The love of Christ overwhelms us at the thought that, if one has died for all, He died that all should no longer live for themselves, but for Him who died and rose for them."[60] The apostle defines the mission in its substantial terms as being overwhelmed, swept along by the memory of Christ's love. This is what "forces" us to the mission and leaves no respite! For whomever is called, chosen by God in Baptism, life's task is not so much to be a father or a mother, a lawyer or a teacher. In all this, your job is to be a prophet, because the mission is first and foremost prophecy, which means "speaking before everyone," spreading the message, the Gospel, the Good News, spreading the Word.

The mission is born of being overwhelmed, as the result of the thought of the love Christ had for us. It is passion, overwhelming passion, for the human glory of Christ that coincides with man's happiness, that gives birth to mission. Being overwhelmed means that you are no longer indifferent. It marks a radical change in the content of your self-awareness. It is the passage to a new content of your self-awareness, in which, instead of the "I," there is a "You." Normally the principle of action is the self; here the principle of action becomes the "You." This passage requires that love be defined by a childlike simplicity that Jesus calls "poverty of spirit," rather than by all the concerns, the stresses, the failures, and the successes from which man naturally draws his motive for following the value of life. One could say that this being overwhelmed, of which St Paul speaks, is the drama of a "forgetting" of self, a self-annihilation for a real *metanoia* to the point of putting the "You" in place of the "I" as the content of self-awareness. For this reason the ideal to follow is the simplicity with which St Peter – though taken unawares – says to Christ: "Yes, You know I love You." Without this *yes*, our own pretensions and illusions come into play.

St Paul has the awareness of an obedience as method, as the source of action. In place of the "I," the subject creating the action becomes a "You"; the "I" sacrifices itself for a You: "I live, not I, but it is Christ who lives in me."[61] It is a fundamental love, wholly gratuitous, without kickbacks or calculations or profits to be had.

In the mission, the offer of oneself to Christ is accomplished, in His living People which is the Church. This happens where He has placed us, in other words in the place and the mode of the charism; this offering is called obedience. In order that men may live no longer for themselves but for Christ, obedience is needed.

Obedience is the essence of the *summum ius*, the summit of God's right over our lives. And this is also the virtue of friendship with Being, the summit of communion with the Mystery.[62] There is no more dramatic word than this. It points to the most dramatic aspect of the moral question: the root of the alternative between one vision of the world and another, between the perception of human consciousness in which the ultimate reality is the Lord, and that in which the lord of reality is what man thinks and feels. What "witnesses" to the Lord is the life of the Christian, insofar as it *demonstrates* this obedience.

The last part of St Paul's phrase we quoted, ("so that they should live for Him who died and rose") highlights the cultural power in which the Christian event expresses itself fully: a new

vision of the world, a new feeling of the world, a totally new effect on the world.

"Living for" indicates the movement of a new culture.

A new culture

What characterizes the cultural dynamics of the Christian Event?
Obedience instead of self-affirmation, living totally in the flesh
but in faith in the Son of God,[63] the fact that One is all and in
Him all are one. Man no longer lives for himself, but for a "You."
He is a new man: "my self is you," I am an Other present. Though
living in the flesh, according to all the levels of his experience of
being man, this new man lives by faith in the Son of God.

The new culture indicates the "for whom" of the new genesis.
The "for whom" is completely changed. It is no longer for ourselves, but for Him who died and rose for us. The "for whom"
indicates the genesis of the new culture. The new man lives for
Him who died, who was killed, who was defeated and who, in
coming back to life, has given proof of His victory over death.[64]
Living for Him is as disturbing as can be. "And that we might
live no longer for ourselves but for Him who died and rose for
us, He sent the Holy Spirit as his first gift to those who believe, to
complete His work on earth and bring us the fullness of grace."[65]

The new culture is a new awareness of oneself and of the common journey;[66] it also implies a new morality, as we mentioned
before, aided by a new correction, a new way of sharing the striving towards the ideal and of forgiving one's weakness regarding
the ideal. This *metanoia* implies the experience of free giving as
the supreme imitation of Christ and of mercy as the Mystery's
way of behaving towards human sin. For one who lives no longer for himself but for God's "You" turns out to be not a selfish
"I" but a self that affirms the free giving of the Creator Mystery,
that belongs totally to the unity that originates in Baptism, unity
of self and unity with others. The "I-You" relationship between
Christ and me is a relationship that carries my whole self in it,
and therefore carries in me all those who share in Christ, as if
they were one (*eis* as St Paul says).[67] With Baptism was born a

new personality which, the more it becomes aware of other human beings also called by Christ, the more it feels one with them ("Don't you know you are members one of another?").[68] Love for others becomes an overwhelming passion for them because they are part of Christ and therefore part of me. This is the new constellation that guides that sky which is God's Holy Church.

Thus arises a true reality of communion that begins and spreads as a whole subject of society, of the world, of human history, of universal history – the Church as the Body of Christ. This human unity, in which He is the foundation, as divine free giving communicated to the chosen creature, has two characteristics. It is all-embracing and Catholic: all-embracing inasmuch as the awareness of this company tends to determine all relationships ("This dear joy / on which all virtue is founded, / whence comes it?"[69] Dante asked himself); Catholic inasmuch as it is a companionship open to everything that emerges and encounters it and thus outstretched to all things. It reaches out tirelessly to the discovery of the truth and to the affirmation of the good in everything.

Do not conform to the mentality of this world

The characteristics of the new culture, generated by those who belong to this communion in history, are reflected in a singular way in the *Letter to the Christians of the West*, by the greatest Bohemian theologian, Josef Zvérina, in which he comments on St Paul's letter to the Romans, 12:1-2. (He had suffered imprisonment for his faith under both the Nazis and Stalin.)

> Brothers,
> You have the presumption of being useful to the Kingdom
> of God assuming as far as possible the *saeculum*, its life,
> its words, its slogans, its way of thinking. But reflect, I beg
> you, what it means to accept this world. Perhaps it means
> that you have gradually lost yourselves in it? Sadly, it seems
> you are doing just that. It difficult these days to find you
> and recognize you in this strange world of yours. Probably
> we still recognize you because in this process you are taking

your time, because you are being assimilated by the world, whether quickly or slowly, but late all the same. We thank you for many things, or rather for almost everything, but we must distinguish ourselves from you in one thing. We have much to admire in you, so we can and must send you this warning.

Do not conform to this world, but transform yourselves by the renewal of your minds, so that you will able to recognize the will of God, what is good, what is pleasing to him, what is perfect (Rom. 12:2). Do not conform! *Me syschematizesthe!* How well this expression reveals the perennial root of the verb: schema. In a nutshell, all schemas, all exterior models are empty. We have to want more, the apostle makes it our duty, "change your way of thinking, reshape your minds" – *metamorfoùsthe tè anakainósei toù noós.* Paul's Greek is so expressive and concrete! He opposes *schèma* or *morphé* – permanent form, to *metamorphé* – change in the creature. One is not to change according to any model that in any case is always out of fashion, but it is a total newness with all its wealth *(anakainósei).* Its not the vocabulary that changes but the meaning *(noùs).*

So not contestation, desacralization, secularization, because this is always little compared with Christian anakaínosis. Reflect on these words and your naïve admiration for revolution, Maoism, and violence (of which, in any case you are incapable) will abandon you.

Your critical and prophetic enthusiasm has already borne fruit, and we cannot indiscriminately condemn you for this. We simply realize, and we tell you sincerely, that we have more esteem for St Paul's calm and discriminating invitation, "Examine yourselves, to see whether you are holding to your faith. Test yourselves. Do you not realize that Jesus Christ is in you?" (2 Cor. 13:5).

We cannot imitate the world precisely because we have to judge it, not with pride and superiority, but with love, just as the Father loved the world (Jn 3:16) and for this reason pronounced judgment on it.

Do not *phroneîn* – think, and in conclusion *hyperphroneîn* –
quibble, but *sophroneîn*, think with wisdom (Cf. Rom. 12:3).
Be wise, so that we can discern the signs of the will and the
time of God. Not the fashion of the moment, but what is
good, honest and perfect.
We write as unwise to you who are wise, as weak men
to you who are strong, as wretched men to you who are
even more wretched! And this is stupid of us because there
are certainly among you some excellent men and women.
But precisely for this reason we need to write foolishly, as
the Apostle Paul taught us, when he took repeated Christ's
words, that the Father has hidden wisdom from those who
know a lot about these things (Lk. 10:21).[70]

Culture is precisely a way of looking, of perceiving, of judging;
that is to say, of evaluating and deciding about everything. It is
the fixing of an ultimate horizon from which the self's awareness
begins its attack on reality and that imbues everything it finds on
the way. The new culture is a vision of the world – from the self
to the Eternal – that starts off from an encounter you have had,
from an event that you are part of, from your coming across a
Presence, not from books you read or ideas you hear. This encounter has a genetic value, since it represents the birth of a new
subject, which arises in a precise place and in a moment of history, where it is nourished and grows as a new personality, with
a unique conception, irreducible to any other; it is given a new
nous, a new knowledge.

When this Presence is at work in all life's relationships, when
all relationships "depend" on this, when they are saved, judged,
coordinated, evaluated, and used in the light of this Presence,
then we have a new culture. This culture springs, therefore, from
the attitude you have towards this exceptional Presence, which
is decisive for life. For this reason St Paul says, "This is your
spiritual worship";[71] it is our culture, a new point of view from
which to look at the world and the whole of reality. When you
look at that Presence with the eyes of a child, whether you are
young or old (it's enough to set aside the ifs and the buts and be

full of the question that nourishes the heart), then you penetrate relationships, whether close or distant, with a light that no one else has, unless he has the same attitude before Christ, before God-made-man, the Word made flesh. "Consider all that is true, all that is good, just, pure, worthy of love and honourable; what comes from virtue and is praiseworthy."[72]

In his comment on the letter to the Romans, Zvèrina stresses that "do not conform" *(me sy-schematìzesthe)* means literally "do not take on the world's schemas,"[73] don't accept the standpoint the world has for looking at things, judging them, and evaluating them. Women, sex, bioethics, politics, art ... it's a question of not using the schema the world uses regarding these things. The Greek verb "do not conform" contains the root of the word "schema." We are surrounded by empty schemas, exterior models. Just think of television and the newspapers that fill the head, eyes, and imagination of everyone who does not defend himself. When is a way of treating people and things not an exterior one? When it participates in the interior reality of which the person and the thing are made – Christ. When is a schema not empty? When it belongs to the Father's plan – which is Christ – in other words, to another culture. A culture is not an empty schema when its origin is something that has happened and from which one cannot tear one's eyes away, a living, unique reality.

Zvèrina goes on, "We cannot copy the world, precisely because we have to judge it." We cannot copy it; certainly not out of pride and superiority, but out of love, just as the Father loved the world and for this reason pronounced His judgment on the world. This is why He sent the word of His truth into the world, which disturbed the world and will disturb it right up to the end.[74] We can't allow ourselves to be sidetracked by exterior models and by empty schemas that are not derived from what things are made of. Because things are made of Christ and the only schema of the world is the Father's plan, and it has a name – Christ. Evil is taking up the schemas of another who is foreign to our new nature.

It is a new culture, one that stands upon new principles and develops new applications. Thus attention is needed so as not to assume the schemas of the world. Let us renew ourselves continually in the novelty, let us penetrate more and more and exalt the novelty that we are. In this way we will have a clear conscience because we shall do what is pleasing to God, what is good, right, and holy: "I exhort you, brothers, to offer your bodies as a living sacrifice, holy and pleasing to God; and this is your spiritual worship."[75] Our culture, our spiritual worship is this offering.

If we reflect on our experience we realize instead how often what prevails is a self-centredness that decides by itself the factors constituting the Event we claim to belong to and that does not spring from us; in place of obedience we impose the affirmation of our own ideas. This is a non-mortification of our pride, it is original sin introducing foreign bodies, induced by something else and accepted by us, into the original simplicity, the creatural simplicity. It is something foreign to the Christian event introducing itself, claiming to be essential to the definition of the event itself, to the extent of not acknowledging it without the presence of this foreign ingredient. "If we bring in liberalism or fascism or capitalism or nationalism, then I'll agree to be a Christian, otherwise no." If we do this we admit exterior restrictions into an irreducibly original Fact, which, to come about, only requires the freedom to accept the Fact as a whole. You accept God on condition that He agree with the predominant cultural ideal, whether it be the humanistic ideal, or that of the Renaissance, or of rationalism.

Today in particular, there is the pretension of identifying the tissue of the Christian Fact not so much with the Event of a Presence, but rather with something that will affirm itself only at the end of time. This is "eschatologism." We could define this as a maniacal exaltation of the final coming of Christ, in which He has nothing to do with the *hic et nunc*, with the here and now (analogous to the maniacal exaltation of reason as the measure of reality, which ends up denying any ultimate consistency of reality itself). Man's effort, from the moment of original sin, would consist in making God have nothing to do with the *hic et nunc*, postponing His action to His last coming.

Eschatologism therefore distracts people from historical responsibility. But in that case, how could we prove that faith is reasonable, given that its reasonableness lies precisely in its capacity to correspond to the human heart's expectation and needs? We couldn't. So eschatologism cannot but be identified with pure fideism.

Instead, for someone who belongs, that is, for the baptized, the supreme formula of the unfolding of the Christ Event is the *hic et nunc*, defined by the circumstances of space and time. As these circumstances develop, belonging to this Event is like the pole that supports a man's tent as he travels through the desert, in history. In this belonging, the tent becomes the dwelling, the temple, the place where God reveals himself continually merciful, and man finds himself continually in Peter's *yes*.

Ecumenism

This new, all-embracing conception of reality developed from the earliest Christian centuries within the Church's experience, perceived as *oikumene*. The Church herself was called *oikumene* (catholic) or *eirene* (peace). The *oikumene* was the vision of the kingdom of Christ that embraces the whole world, all times, and all space. With the word *oikumene* the human, social, and cultural subject was established, capable of embracing the whole universe.

We have used the word "culture" to define the profound way in which the human heart gives rise to an overall image of relationship with itself, with people, and with things. But this cannot derive solely from the enigmatic depth of our elementary experience, with its broad range of needs, interests, and original requirements, so rich but still fragmented and so hard to decipher – a baffling condition that makes man forever restive.[76] This restlessness is witnessed by the bewilderment found in our modern-day mentality, unable to overcome the divisions and contradictions, which are an inevitable consequence of a cultural conception in which the starting point is always the focus on a detail, idolatrously exalted to qualify everything. It is from this that falsehood and violence inevitably arise.

The Christian term that so well expresses originality and cultural development in the totality of its factors is "ecumenism,"[77] in its original etymological sense, which derives from *oikumene*. It means that the Christian view reverberates with a momentum that makes you able to exalt all the good that is present in all that you meet, a momentum that makes you acknowledge your participation in that plan that will be perfectly realized in eternity and that has been revealed in Christ.

Ecumenism starts from the Event of Christ, which is the Event of truth in all that is, of all time and space, of history. It is truth happening in the world – the Word has become flesh, the truth has become a human presence in history and remains in the present. This Presence invades – tends to invade – all of reality. When you are clearly conscious of the supreme truth that is the face of Christ, then you see something good in all you meet. Ecumenism is therefore not a generic tolerance that can leave the other person yet a stranger, but a love for the truth that is present in anyone, even if only a fragment of it. Every time a Christian meets a new reality he faces it positively, because it carries some echo of Christ, some echo of the truth.

Nothing is excluded from this positive embrace. This universality is the result of the missionary experience implied in the choice that God makes of the baptized and in the destiny for which one is chosen. The task of the baptized is the universal mission that God communicates to him as a sharing in the great mission of Christ. So the more he is committed to this mission the more he is also committed to discover the good that persists in all things, the fragment or the reflection of truth. Since I am part of the reality of Christ, I look at the mountains, the morning and the evening, all reality, looking first for the ultimate root in everything I see. And the conviction that the truth is in me and with me makes me extremely positive about everything. Not equivocal, but positive. If there is the tiniest bit of truth in something I affirm it. In this way a "critical" approach to reality is born, according to what St Paul says, "pànta dokimàzete, tò kalòn katéchete,"[78] "sift everything and keep what is of value," what is beautiful, what is true, what corresponds to the original criterion of your heart.

The Christ Event is the true source of the critical attitude, since it does not mean finding the limitations of things, but discovering their value. Along these lines, an episode in an apocryphal writing speaks of Jesus walking through the fields and seeing the rotting carcass of a dead dog. St Peter, who was in front, says, "Master step around it," but Jesus went ahead and stopped before the carcass and said, "What beautiful white teeth!"[79] It was the only good thing in that rotten carcass. Limitations are notable and strike us all very easily, whereas the true value of things is discovered only by those who have the perception of being and of goodness, those who are able to bring out being and make it loved, without obliterating, cutting off, or denying, because to be critical is not to be hostile to things, but to love them. So you cannot be truly critical if you are not at peace through a love that possesses us and that we possess. Only if you are totally possessed by a love, only if you acknowledge that you belong to the love of Christ "brimming over with peace,"[80] are we like children who walk without fear in a dark forest.

It is the Event of Christ that creates the new culture and gives rise to true criticism. Valuing the good in all things, however little or however much, commits us to create a new civilization, to love a new construction. Thus a new culture is born, as the bond uniting all the fragments of good that are found, in striving to give them importance and to make them work. You stress the positive, despite its limitations, and you leave the rest to the Father's mercy. "The Lord is not slow to fulfill his promise, as some think, but He uses patience towards you, not wanting anyone to perish, but that all should have the means to repent."[81] It is not that God is slow in coming, but He waits so that in His patience everyone should be able to bear fruit for his soul. The world has to be won over to Christianity in the end by this word that sums up everything: "mercy." The capacity for mercy is expressed as sensitivity to the good, as the certainty that with the power of Christ the good wins over: "I love you God, my strength";[82] "I am capable of all things in Him in whom is my strength."[83]

So there is one single source of a positive view of everything. On the other hand whoever is attached to a partial identification, to his own truth, cannot avoid looking at everything while defending his own position, unless he is totally skeptical or nihilist. Often the leaders of peoples, those with various claims to responsibility, if they are filled with common sense, favour a certain "ecumenism," because they are terrified of war and violence, which are inevitable consequences when someone asserts only himself. So it seems that joining together, trying to respect each others' identity might represent the realisation of *eirene*. But this is not peace, it is ambiguity. For at best this ends up as tolerance, in other words radical indifference. Thus the term "ecumenism," as it is proclaimed these days, seems to be the best expression of the good will of those who are in good faith, and are leaders of people, whether they are religious or political leaders. This "ecumenism" understood as a confraternity of the various philanthropic enterprises for building the world, turns out to be the chief enemy of the Christian identity. For at best it is an attempt at tolerance where each one is looking for his own interests and takes from the others what he finds useful. But if each one is only looking for his own particular interests, in the end they will all see each other as potential enemies to be defended against. For in the face of what interests us most, we cease to be tolerant.

Instead Catholic ecumenism is open to everyone and everything, down to the smallest nuances, ready to exalt what has a distant affinity with the truth with all possible generosity. If someone has discovered the real truth, Christ, he proceeds confidently in every kind of encounter, sure of finding a piece of himself in everyone.

True ecumenism keeps on discovering new things, so that there is never a total repetition: one is drawn on by an all-encompassing wonder before beauty. From beauty, time and time again are born images of unsuspected possibilities for repairing the ruined houses and building new ones.[84] This openness has us find ourselves at home with anyone who preserves a scrap of truth, and feel at ease everywhere. It is the concept of catholicity not understood geographically (as it has been since 1500), but ontologically defined by truth.

The *Imitation of Christ* says, "Ex uno Verbo omnia et unum loquuntur omnia, et hoc est Principium quod et loquitur nobis."[85] ("From one single Word everything, and one single Word cries out everything. And this Word is the Principle that speaks in us.") It's impossible to find another culture that defines everything with such a unitary and powerful embrace, that leaves nothing out. Jacopone da Todi in the eleventh century said that everything happens so that we all go together into the *"regno celesto che compie omne festo / che'l cor ha bramato"*[86] (the heavenly kingdom that perfects every feast / that the heart has longed for). And again, in the finest verse of Italian literature, *"Amor, amore, omne cosa conclama"*[87] ("Love, love, all things together cry out"). The word love is to be understood in its ultimate sense, as synonymous with Christ, with God who has bent down over us and embraced us. All things together cry out the truth. All things – the flowers of the field, the leaves on the trees, all the pine needles on earth (who knows how God can count them all?).

5   ENTERING INTO REALITY AS A WHOLE

This conception of culture and ecumenism requires a totally new approach to education. Christian formation has the aim of educating the human person in all his dimensions. Christian companionship, understood as the dwelling place of the human, encourages the person persuasively, pedagogically, and systematically to compare himself with reality up to its furthest frontiers, reawakening and sustaining the set of questions and original points of evidence that constitute our heart. This teaches us to sift everything and keep what is good; in other words, it educates us.

What does it mean to educate?

To educate means to help the human soul to enter into reality as a whole.[88] There is a starting point that makes this definition more understandable: reason is awareness of reality, as it emerges from experience, according to the totality of its factors.[89] Without this totality we could not speak of rationality. If reason becomes a definition of reality while neglecting totality, then it is presumption, pretension, the inappropriate dilation of the sphere of knowledge, reduction, constriction, a premise for obstructing freedom. Taking in reality as a whole – this is why man must always feel, sincerely and humbly, that he is searching. The more lively and humble this quest, the more intelligent its outcome will be, since man will involve in his engagement, in his effort, all that he finds positive and agreeable. Someone who deceives himself into thinking that he has already found everything and has nothing new to discover risks discarding along his way the very encounters that can be the most meaningful. For this reason someone who "already knows" that his own religion is enough will never meet Jesus Christ, even if Christ were to knock on his door, sit down at his table, and speak for two or three hours, as he did with John and Andrew. He will never understand!

To educate someone is to help him to understand the factors of reality as they go on multiplying till they become a whole that will always remain the true endpoint of his action. You do not need to be Leopardi, with his hymn *To his Woman*[90] to understand that the woman you have found is the beginning of a journey towards a horizon that lies within the relationship with her, but is greater than that relationship and goes beyond it. Thus the woman is the symbol of a higher ideal of goodness, of beauty, and of love. This broader horizon must preside over all man's activities, otherwise that activity is constricted, as a use of reality, and therefore as a gift to society for everyone's benefit.

It seems abstract to speak of "reality as a whole"; but anyone who has not perceived the love with which this word reaches him and the concreteness in which it can and must be expressed, is far away from that "reality" he thinks he is master of. For example, a man could tell his children, "Look at me, look how I work!" But if his children have come across a group of friends who have woken them up through a proper education, they answer him (or think to themselves if they can't quite tell him outright), "OK

Dad, but you can't be otherwise, because you've been brought up that way, you've taught yourself that way, but things are different now, they need a new approach. Something new is needed!" To educate means to keep alive this search for "something new," because the horizon that moves man, in all that he does, is the infinite. In his actions, man opens himself up to a horizon that is within what he identifies as his aim; but he transcends it, he goes beyond it. Thus everything is outstripped by the relationship that constitutes man's heart – the relationship with the infinite.

An action, any action whatsoever (St Paul says, "eating or drinking," the most everyday example he could have used; "waking," how complicated! and "sleeping," how simple, so near to nothingness; "living or dying") is for the human glory of Christ.[91] Man is related to the eternal Mystery of the Trinity, which we know through the humanity of Christ. It is the relationship with Christ's humanity that allows us to keep our eyes and our hearts open to the real aim for which our father and mother conceived us, for which our mother gave birth to us: to live the relationship with the Infinite. This is why Dante said, "Everyone confusedly perceives a good in which his soul may rest and he desires it, and everyone strives to attain it."[92] In his life man strives to verify all the implications of the Infinite, in terms of the fullness that this presence suggests to his heart.

Educating in freedom

You cannot educate someone unless you appeal to his freedom, by calling it to action and responsibility. Freedom defines the self: it is already all there when man says "I," it is all there in this "I" he pronounces; but freedom is also something in which one has to be educated.[93]

Usually one thinks – bitterly and sadly – of freedom as the absence of bonds. It is a temptation that has faced men of all times. When the apostles heard Jesus affirm that marriage was indissoluble they said, "If that's the case, then it's better not to marry!"[94] If freedom is the absence of bonds, then it means, for example, that my relationship with my wife is at the mercy of my whims, and vice-versa. Or we think of freedom as doing just what we like. Existentially, however, we verify that it is not. How we get alarmed when our children, even when they are still young, want to travel their own road, want to use their time as they like, want to choose according to their interests! This is the aspect that St Augustine grasped when he observed that man always follows the *delectatio victrix*,[95] the victorious attraction, the strongest attraction. For the predominant mentality, following this attraction usually means following one's instinct, because normally what is strongest is instinct, reaction. This is always the choice that the intelligence makes to suit one's own convenience or interests. So is freedom simply to do what you like? No, this is not freedom. Experientially, even psychologically, man feels free, truly free, not when he is doing what he likes, but when he is satisfied, when something satisfies him, *(satis facit)*, completes or fulfills him. But what can complete or fulfill man? "Quid animo satis?"[96] St Francis of Assisi asked. What can be enough for the soul? Only relationship with the infinite!

Freedom is not what justifies man's actions within the terms with which he measures reality. When man makes himself "the measure of all things," then it is as if what he cannot measure does not exist. Freedom is not the employment of a measure that confines reality within four walls, whether they be as small as those of a room or as huge as those of the universe, because the universe is still a room, Leopardi's "earthly room."[97] Just as you can suffocate in a tiny room, if you are ill in bed for days and days, you can suffocate while looking at the sky, the earth and the sea, if you look at them as limited. Death is the symbol of all this – the supreme limit. Freedom is not the activity that man carries out while making himself the measure of things, or a space in which he can be master. Freedom is adherence to reality that never stops being investigated, which the eye never ceases to penetrate, even were we to live a thousand years. In fact, after a thousand years we would be even more pervaded by the sense of awe that comes as we think of our limitation before the immensity of the origin of things, of the incommensurability of the Mystery – of things and of the universe as mystery.

Freedom is that level of nature in which nature becomes capable of relationship with the infinite, in which nature says "You" to this ineffable, incomprehensible, unimaginable presence without which nothing is conceivable, because nothing makes itself. There is no evidence more imposing than this. In this instant, the most evident thing to me, according to my maturity, more evident than the fact that I am, that I exist, is that I am not making myself. The most vivid aspect of the perception of my existence is that I don't make myself:[98] I don't give myself even a single hair of my head, as Jesus said.[99] True freedom is therefore the capacity that man has to adhere to being – not only to decide, but to approve of being and adhere to it.[100] Thus, the relationship between the self and all that surrounds it, between the self and the universe, comes to be conceived as a marriage, a profound union – it is a universal spousal image.

Now precisely this freedom, all intent on embracing reality more and more, becomes a factor of recovery when your knowledge of things, and therefore your approach to what you have in hand, is blocked within the narrowness of your own measure, when, in other words, you act without the sense of that "beyond" that lies within and behind all that man takes hold of. For freedom makes us more attentive to every reminder and every correction, in the etymological sense we have stressed (sustaining each other). The more you love perfection in the reality of things, the more you love the persons for whom you do things and the more you love the society for which you work, whatever kind of work you do, then the more you want to be perfected by correction. This is the poverty in possessing things that makes man an actor, a creator, and a protagonist.

As well as being a factor of continual recovery, freedom is also a creative impulse. If it is relationship with the infinite, it draws from the infinite an unfailing will to create. Just as everything can be corrected, so everything can be created in obedience to God. This creator instinct is what qualifies freedom in a more positive and experientially appealing way. A society is made by the assertion of this creativity of which man's freedom is capable.

We can now point out the factors of a true adult education and of human freedom affirmed seriously, an education and a freedom conceived according to their profound, original meaning.

Educating in social life

Education in perfect freedom expresses also itself as education in social life. This gives room to approximation because of the risk present in every contingent moment. Education in social life implies four basic points: education in labour and works, freedom of education, education in justice, and education in political life.

a) Labour and works

Christian companionship educates us to enter into the whole of reality through the manipulation of reality itself, through work (the work of housewives and mothers with their children, the work of big managers or of those who have even more substantial power). It is above all in the approach to day-to-day circumstances implicit in his work that man goes more deeply into the original dynamic that, in continuous impact with reality, brings out the needs that make up his self (the need for good, for truth, and for beauty). This dynamic, as a continuous discovery, is a true work within work, or more precisely the true work of life.

In work, man strives to project himself, his plan, and his ideal into time and space. For Christianity, human work is the slow beginning of man's dominion over things, a lordship to which he aspires by realizing the image of God, the "Lord."[101] Precisely through work reality is transformed and shaped by man. After original sin, reality is no longer directly ordered to its end as it was in the beginning; it has become ambiguous. How can it come to be shaped once more according to truth? Where do we start? We start from the human friendship that is established among those who gather together in the name of Christ, and is called the Church. For it was the Christ Event that gave back to the world its true meaning. Christians collaborate in this way in the Father's plan for the world. The Christian community, with the active grace of the Spirit, collaborates in the plan of redemption through work. In this way work becomes an expansion of the Mystery of salvation in every moment and activity, in the context of each one's personal function and situation.

Sincere respect for work makes it intolerable that others cannot work, because education in freedom is abstract if a man has no work to learn or to do. It is in carrying out my work that I understand that I am free, that my freedom is respected, or, on the contrary, that everything is hindered, restricted, inadequately defined, or predefined. Education in freedom is impossible without the opportunity to have a job. An unemployed person suffers a serious attack on his self-awareness. Man does not know himself by reflecting on himself (this requires an objectivity of which few are capable, possible through a proper philosophical preparation) but he perceives his value, his faculties, his capabilities, by doing, by working, *in actu exercito*, as St Thomas Aquinas says.[102] A man gets to know himself only in action, in the course of action, while he is in action. So if he has no work in life, man has less knowledge of himself. He tends to lose the sense of his life. We said that freedom is not simply being able to choose, but the need and the desire for the infinite, a striving towards the infinite. This infinite destiny we are made for is realized through day-to-day needs in which your own need for the infinite is articulated and becomes concrete. Daily needs provoke us to move towards destiny. Thus the need for a particular thing is the way that infinity touches us and makes us react. This reaction, if it comes from a self that is engaged and not bent just on comfort, will lead us to deal with the need naturally in some sort of systematic way. This can lead to an "enterprise." An enterprise appears as the concretization in a given moment – therefore eminently open to criticism and refinement – of an ideal that cannot fail to be acknowledged as greater than any solution conceived and realized. The origin of an enterprise is the attempt to give a systematic answer, in terms of the the image suggested by the ideal, to a need that you meet at a particular time, on a particular day.

But, just as we cannot be born and cannot live on our own, so we cannot find answers to our own needs (whatever they may be, even the most personal ones) unless we are in a companion-ship, with the help of a companionship. No one can tackle a need as systematically as our natural life requires if he is alone. The action that creates an enterprise is by its very nature intent on answering the need of the person and in that sense it is also in-tent on efficiency, combatting everything that could compromise it. The work for an enterprise aimed at answering the need of an individual is characterized by this ultimate sociality of our pres-ence in the world and, therefore by the need for companionship. This is a great thing!

So we are more and more deeply attached to the figure of God who became one of us and has become present for all times pre-cisely within a companionship: "I shall be with you all days, till the end of time."[103] The human factors of the question (striving towards destiny, commitment to the needs and the companion-ship necessary) are exalted by our admiration, by the *memory*, that is to say, by the recognition of Christ present.

Work is thus the final synthesis of the relationship between the "I" and the reality that provokes it, projecting it towards destiny, in other words, towards Christ, and is also the synthesis between this provocation by reality and the relationship with all those who acknowledge the Lord – our destiny, which has become a presence.

What characterizes enterprises generated by an authentic re-sponsibility must be realism and prudence. Realism is tied up with the fact that truth is the conforming of the intellect to real-ity,[104] while prudence – which in the *Summa* of St Thomas is defined[105] as a correct criterion in the things we do – is the meas-ure of the truth of things, before being a measure of the ethical aspect of goodness. Precisely because of this need for realism and prudence, an enterprise becomes the sign of a capacity for imagination, for sacrifice, and for openness. In this free and cre-ative social experience are rooted the strength and the durability of personal responsibility, even in the face of power. Personal responsibility is safeguarded and affirmed in the acknowledged primacy of society vis-a-vis the State. By this primacy we mean

giving value to the original fabric created by dynamic relationships between the natural communities and between the various
movements present in society. By creating enterprises and aggre-
gations, the overall movement of persons gives rise to intermedi-
ate communities, which express the freedom of the individuals
empowered by associative forms.

b) Freedom of education

Freedom has its most privileged expression in its ability to educate. The first implication of the words "freedom of education"
stresses its value as an indispensable condition for full human
expressivity. This is why John Paul II said, "Without freedom
there can be no culture,"[106] no authentic cultural development.
Second, it indicates the intrinsic dynamic of the educative process. This is why we speak of the "risk of education," because the
educational process is a risk, precisely because it brings into play
the freedom of both the educator and the one being educated.[107]
If this freedom is inherent to education, then we can understand
how the essential condition for dignity in educational development and in a culture lies in your ability to value your own cultural position and to freely communicate it to others. If one is to
educate in freedom there must be freedom in education.

Concern for education is surely the greatest sign of the will
to give and of loving passion for man. In concrete life, the first
freedom is not, so to say, towards myself, but towards the one I
love – my child, my brother, and, from a Christian standpoint,
even towards a complete stranger. As regards someone you love,
how desirable is this freedom to educate, in educating, in helping
a person to enter into the whole of reality! In a mature man, this
desire is almost stronger than a mother's love for her child.

To transform the world, we must bring our humanity to fulfillment in all its dimensions; but a true humanity cannot develop in
a regime of constrictions. Today there is much talk of pluralism
in education, but in practice it is not tolerated; so much so that
Pope Paul VI went as far as to speak of "cultural terrorism," to
point out how serious had become the situation in which the
whole process of education and culture is enslaved by power.

Without freedom, there can be neither true human education nor
authentic culture. So education and culture, which are born free,
must spread in a regime of freedom.

c) Justice

In a free society, true justice is a source of peace, which is the sign
of true belonging to God; but our justice is not enough. "This
kind of abuse of the idea of justice and the practical distortion of
it show how far human action can deviate from justice itself, even
when it is being undertaken in the name of justice. Not in vain did
Christ challenge His listeners, faithful to the doctrine of the Old
Testament, for their attitude which was manifested in the words:
'An eye for an eye and a tooth for a tooth.' "[108] This was the form
of distortion of justice at that time; and today's forms continue
to be modelled on it. It is obvious that in the name of an alleged
justice (for example, historical justice or class justice) the neighbour is sometimes destroyed, killed, deprived of liberty, or stripped
of fundamental human rights."[109] For there to be peace in social
life it is necessary that justice be seriously and honestly practised,
respecting first of all those rights of the individual, of the person,
that have characterized the history of jurisprudence in civil society.
There is civil society when jurisprudence respects these original
and irreducible needs that cannot be sacrificed by any norm or by
any power. Justice cannot be affirmed by treading on the values
with which the life of a people is woven, destroying its welfare
and the possibility of a view to the future, leading astray the most
attentive hearts. It was exactly this historical experience that led to
the affirmation: *summum ius, summum iniuria.*

This affirmation does not underestimate human effort, and
does not weaken the meaning of the order that man tries to establish as an answer to the natural needs for justice present in his
heart. On the one hand it contests the abstract and therefore vio-
lent claim of an absolute measure of justice, one disengaged from
the consideration of the totality of the factors that constitute
the good of the person and the common good, and on the other
hand it indicates the need for a reference that is not exhausted
within the bounds of human measure, but draws from the power

of Christ, who is the true answer and ideal image of the human need for justice. Moreover this becomes glaringly evident with the realistic realization, continually suggested by life experience, that in order for there to be true justice, human good will and consistency are not enough. Who is able to be consistent? No one! For perfection is not the result of a consistency. Even for justice, perfection comes from the relationship with destiny made man, with a "you," living and present in the complexity of human existence. So St Paul says, with great realism and foresight, "Now it is evident that no man is justified before God by the law; for 'He who through faith is righteous shall live.'"[110]

d) Political life[111]

In his relentless effort to know and embrace the real, so as to make it more in keeping with the ideal impetus that moves him, man has to deal with power. By power we mean what Romano Guardini, in one of his books,[112] indicates as the factor defining the common goal and the organization of things needed for achieving it. Now, either power is determined by the will of serving God's creature as it evolves (that is to say to serve man, culture and the consequent praxis), or it tends to reduce human reality to what it has previously decided as its own image of the evolution of reality and of history. As a rule, in this second case, power is identified with a State that posits itself as the source of all rights and thus tends to reduce man, as *Gaudium et spes* tells us, to "a speck of matter or an anonymous citizen of the earthly city."[113]

If power aims exclusively at achieving its own image of the real, it must seek to govern human desires; for desire is the emblem of freedom, because it expresses man's original openness to the horizon of totality. The problem of power is that of securing for itself the maximum consensus from a mass of people that is more and more conditioned as regards its needs. Thus the mass media, the main vehicle of secularized culture, become tools for the tenacious inculcation of certain desires and for the obliteration or exclusion of others. Man's desires, and therefore his values, undergo an essential and systematic reduction. As John Paul II observed in the encyclical *Dives in Misericordia*, "This is the tragedy of our time:

the loss of freedom of conscience on the part of whole peoples achieved by the cynical use of mass media by those in power."[114]

What then is the consequence of all this? The social panorama becomes more and more uniform and grey. It is the great "homogenization" of which Pier Paolo Pasolini spoke.[115] We could describe the situation with this formula: P μ I. Power is directly proportional to impotence. Power becomes high-handedness before an impotence brought about through the systematic reduction of desires, of needs and of values.

Vàclav Bèlohradsky, one of the first signatories of *Charta 77*,[116] said in an interview:

> European tradition means never being able to live beyond
> the bounds of one's conscience, reducing it to an anonymous
> apparatus like the law or the State. This 'firmness' of the con-
> science is a heritage of the Greek, Christian, bourgeois trad-
> ition. The irreducibility of conscience to institutions is under
> threat in the age of mass-media, of totalitarian States and of the
> general computerization of society. For it's all too easy for us to
> imagine institutions so perfectly organized as to impose any-
> thing they do as legitimate. You only need an efficient organ-
> ization at your disposal to legitimize anything at all. We could
> summarize the essence of what is threatening us as follows: the
> States program the citizens; the industries program the consum-
> ers; the publishing houses program the readers, etc. Little by
> little, society becomes something the State produces for itself.[117]

The levelling-out of desire gives rise to bewilderment in the young and cynicism in adults. Then what alternative is there to this general feebleness? Voluntarism with no breath and no horizon, without genius and with no space of freedom – a moralism of dependence on the State, conceived as the ultimate source of consistency for the human flow of history.

If politics is the set of models and methods for tackling problems of human life in society, then a dramatic comparison between these models must be developed to establish who should lead the people in each moment. A political organization that would tend to suffocate rather than favour and defend social creativity would inevitably contribute towards generating or sustaining a State that domineers society. Such a State would be reduced to serving the plans of those in power. Personal and social responsibility would be evoked only to arouse consensus on what has already been planned. And even morality would be conceived and acclaimed to serve the status quo, which would, perhaps, be called "peace."

Pasolini bitterly suggested that a State of power (that is to say, a State as a power set-up), such as we see forming in many situations today, is practically unchangeable. Such a State ends up leaving space for utopia, aware that utopia cannot stand the test of time, or to individual nostalgia, aware of its impotence to bring about any change.

On the contrary, true politics is that which defends a newness of life in the present, capable of changing the power establishment. Politics must decide therefore whether to favour society exclusively as an instrument of manipulation by the State, an object of its power, or to favour a State that is truly "secular," that is to say, at the service of living society according to the Thomistic concept of "common good," continually and vigorously referred to by the Church's Magisterium.

Politics, then, must be in an ideal position, in other words, one that explicitly recognizes man's original link with his destiny. Without an ideal position, man is incapable of a certainty that can develop into building something. We have already noted that a people are formed by means of a particular event that took place in time, and are united by an ideal that they pursue (recognized and sensed to a greater or lesser degree). Otherwise what we have is not a people, but a flock of sheep. And the greatest temptation for those in power is to make the people into a flock of sheep, that is to say to deprive them of every ideal, while preserving all the exterior forms. "O people of Italy, old slothful titan, / I called you vile to your face, you called out to me Bravo."[118] A political program that is interested not in an ideal position but in "success" by means of conquered power, is an enemy of the people. A political program concerned with an ideal position sets in motion an educational process, bringing about a wider aspiration of freedom for all, and therefore greater creativity and vision. These days, there are no great creators, and it's more and more difficult for them to arise, because there is little space for creativity.

Politics needs to be practised by people who have a real interest in man. This is a duty that binds us in our choice of who should represent us. It is an essential premise. Then they can speak of economy, railways, armed forces, and secret services; but first they must show they have a real interest in man. This is what makes politics an activity that collaborates with the plan of God, the Lord; in other words, the only political schema whose power is irresistible positivity.

The characteristic of the new people born of the Event of Christ, in approaching day-to-day circumstances, in the efforts, the risks, and sacrifices this implies, is a free giving that tries to imitate the superabundance and the grace with which Christ came and has remained among us, a free giving that is a source of gladness, amidst sacrifices, contradictions, and pain. A passage of the Ambrosian Liturgy says, "*Notam faciam gloriam nominis mei in laetitia cordis eorum*," "I will make known my presence through the gladness of their hearts,"[119] and another states explicitly the link between this gladness and the event of a new people: "*In simplicitate cordis mei laetus obtuli universa et sic ingenti gaudio populum tuum vidi tibi offerre donaria*," ("In the simplicity of my heart I was glad to offer you everything and thus I saw your people offer you gifts with great joy.")[120] It is the echo of Jesus's last recommendation, "I have told you these things that my joy may be in you and that your joy be complete."[121] And Jesus was speaking of this joy just a few hours before he was murdered.

The Event of Christ has to do with the present, so much so that it effectively changes the present, more effectively than all the social resources imaginable, because "joy" or "gladness" cannot be the aim of any social resource, however newly conceived. The supreme duty of one who has faith, of the protagonist of history in this new people, is precisely that of demonstrating, of witnessing the truth of the Christ Event through a gladness that endures, even in the worst circumstances of life, since gladness is the exceptional, dizzying epitome of a change that has taken place, a change that reveals a new ontology.

4

The Day of Christ, the Day of Mercy

I THE DAY OF CHRIST

Only mercy permits a people to journey forward, because only in mercy is it possible to build a people when we can no longer imagine the true road. Only God can look at man keeping all of his factors in mind. He is the only one who can, because original sin has even "slowed down" our reason. Though life remains a great enigma, at the peak of his self-perception, man can manage to sense the need for "forgiveness," the need that being, that reality be "forgiveness" – as expressed by Pascoli in his poem *Two Orphans*. "Now we are better ... now that there is no one who is pleased with us; that there is no one to forgive us."[1] The heart cannot conceive of such an "ultimate" forgiveness. The furthest step that reason can ascribe to man is identified rather by the word "justice," or, in a culture influenced by Christianity, with an affirmation of hope, as in the verses of Ada Negri: "Now, God whom I have always loved, I love you knowing I love you; and the ineffable certainty that everything was justice, even the pain, everything was good, even my evil, everything for me You were and are, makes me tremble with a joy greater than death."[2] Here is a hope that contradicts the dark desperation that man succumbs to.

If every hour of history is the hour of Christ's human glory that happens through the conscious offering of the believers, there will come a day that no one knows (neither the angels of God, nor the Son, but only the Father)[3] when the definitive revelation of the Mystery will take place, as the valuing of every good the Father has generated, the Son has assumed, and the Spirit has made fruitful. All the good, even the furtive move stirred up in the almost unconscious darkness of human endeavours in history, will not be erased by God who, as the summit of Being, cannot contradict Himself by annihilating one single instant of good. It will be the day of the triumph of Christ, who will hand over everything to the Father, so that the Father may be "all in all."[4]

The day of the radiant and definitive glory of Christ is the exact opposite of the chilling vision of the nihilist.[5] This final victory of Christ is certain, though how it will occur remains a total mystery that the humble heart of the believer accepts, singing praise to God in the fearful acknowledgment that he cannot conceive how the Father's forgiveness can embrace the prodigal son (and when you are a prodigal son, it seems as though you have never come back!).

In Rembrandt's famous painting,[6] the prodigal son is the mirror image of the Father. The Father's face is full of sorrow at the son's error, at his denial, full of a sorrow that flows back into forgiveness. Human imagination can reach this point. But the most spectacular and mysterious thing is that the Father's face is the mirror image of the prodigal son. In Rembrandt's painting, the Father is in a position that mirrors the son – in Him is reflected the son's sorrow, the despair overcome, the destruction prevented, the happiness about to rekindle, in the instant in which it is about to rekindle, when goodness triumphs. Goodness triumphs in the prodigal son because he weeps for his mistake. But goodness triumphs in the Father: this is the concept of mercy, which man cannot manage to understand, or to speak of.[7] The Father's face is the reflection of the son.[8] And the Father's face *is* mercy, because it is pity for the one who has gone wrong and is there, turned towards the one who is coming back.

But if mercy is such an important part of the Mystery, it is through the Son, Word of God, Mirror of the Father, that this is revealed to man. For it is the Word of the Father who puts on human nature so as to reveal to man all that the Mystery is for him. So in history mercy has a name – Jesus Christ.[9]

Man's surrender to the Father's mercy becomes true total surrender to the cross of the Son, who says in our favour, "Father, forgive them for they do not know what they are doing."[10] Man can only surrender. In this surrender he experiences the love of the Mystery as a power that "absorbs" him and re-creates him. It is an absolute trust, an absolute surrender, a surrender comparable to that of Our Lady in the instant in which "the angel left her."[11]

In the terrifying darkness of total surrender to the Father, Christ, the mercy of the Infinite, offered His life for every man,[12] even for Judas, as Péguy recalls, though in the limitation of human vision.[13]

If Christ is the protagonist of the "last day," the day of Christ's triumph will therefore be the day of mercy. One would even say that the word "mercy" should be removed from the dictionary because it does not exist in the world of man, there is nothing that corresponds to it. Mercy is at the origin of forgiveness, it is forgiveness affirmed at its origin, which is infinite. It is forgiveness as Mystery.

2 MERCY IS MYSTERY

Mercy is not a human word. It is identical with Mystery; it is the Mystery from which everything comes, upon which everything is supported, and in which everything will end, inasmuch as it is communicated to human experience. The description of the prodigal son is the description of mercy that invades and penetrates the life of that young man. The concept of forgiveness, with a certain proportion between mistakes and punishments, is in some way conceivable for human reason, but not this limitless forgiveness that is mercy. Being forgiven arises here from something absolutely incomprehensible to man, from the Mystery; in other words, from mercy. It is what cannot be understood that ensures the exceptionality of what can be understood, because God's life is love, *caritas*,[14] absolute free giving, love without profit, humanly "without reasons." Humanly, it appears almost as an injustice or something irrational – precisely because we do not see any reasons for it; because mercy is proper to Being, to the infinite Mystery.

The reality of mercy is the supreme opportunity that Christ and the Church have for making His Word reach man, not just as a mere echo of this word in man. How does the infinite Mystery behave towards us? By comprehending and forgiving everything! And man has always rebelled at this;[15] from the start he rebelled against the fact that an Other, albeit the Mystery who hade made him, should be the reason for what he was doing. Adam and Eve wanted to affirm their selves against the divine self. The whole of philosophy, in as much as it is irreligious or, at least contrary to the Christian God, is a continuous rebellion in the name of a supposed "dignity" of reason and of God's perfection to be respected. It is a refusal of how God manifests Himself. "And if I want to be good to everyone, are you to complain to me, you, who only need to think of what I have forgiven you? Think of what I have forgiven you!"[16] But His being good to all makes our thoughts explode. It would be better if He were to make us children, it would make us understand at the age of fifty the taste of being children, of being children before their father and mother.

"May the peace of God reign in your hearts," St Paul wrote to the Colossians.[17]

"But, I've done this and that!" It is our cowardice, our pettiness and pride that wishes to impose upon God's infinite liberality and magnanimity. For even the fact that it seems irrational to us, since we cannot demonstrate it, is truly part of the Mystery. God instead overtakes us on all sides because, precisely through the astonishment that overwhelms us at His mercy, He causes us to feel, first, a sorrow that we have never felt before; but not an exasperated, selfish sorrow, such as when we feel our dignity is hurt and we feel horror at ourselves. Here we can understand how the one who hates God and wants, irrationally, to challenge Him, gives no respite to our life, and tries to drag us, too, into his wicked lie – he is the "father of lies," Satan,[18] as Jesus said. It's rather a matter of discovering the truth in us, who are small and weak in the face of the Mystery of Being. "We should not wonder if weakness is weak."[19] It is better to be children in the hands of mercy.

So we do not offer any objections – none of us is merciful; but we must try to be. How is this possible?

In virtue of the revelation of His mercy – which would seem to sanction all human behaviour, but it does not – God fills us with sorrow for the evil that we were not even aware of before.[20] How could a man be positive, after having done certain things? Yet Peter says *yes* at once, before going back to consider all his misdeeds. He feels no more horror at what he had done, because horror sets man once more in the foreground. What imposes itself is sorrow for one's own sins, as the historic beginning of a love that waits to be answered. This is sorrow. Man is glad because God is alive – his is a sorrow full of gladness, but it is still sorrow, sorrow at oneself. All the same, it is a sorrow that laughs, like the sorrow of a child who has fallen down and whose face is wet with tears, and weeps for the pain he feels, but smiles at his father and mother.

Second, through our astonishment at His mercy, He makes us desire to be like Him. Even people who have no interest in the Church or in morality desire to be like Him! They begin really to forgive their enemies, those who do them harm; so we can understand how Job, before the enemies who had destroyed everything he had, could say, "The Lord gave, the Lord has taken away; blessed be the name of the Lord."[21] When we get up in the morning, feeling the forgiveness that renews our lives, we also feel like saying, "Lord, help me to be like You!" For Jesus had already told His disciples, "Be merciful, as your heavenly Father is merciful."[22] This seems to go against good sense, but only up to a certain point, because it is desire that defines the soul of the new man. We are not truly human if we do not wish to be merciful like our heavenly Father. The question is whether or not we really desire it. So the miracle of mercy is the desire to change. And this implies acceptance, because otherwise it would not be desire for change, but pretension and presumption, and it would never become entreaty to an Other, it would not be trust in an

Other. This desire defines the present, the instant of the man who is a sinner. The miracle is accepting oneself and entrusting oneself to an Other present so as to be changed, standing before Him and begging.

Entreaty is the whole expression of man now, in the instant. So there is no need to be afraid of anything, not even of yourself. And we feel like children whom the Father bends down to pick up.[23] Man becomes truly a child held in his Father's arms.[24] A person in his poverty, astonished by the mysterious perfection of God, Father, Son and Spirit, asks to be like Him. And this is not a bold presumption, but a realistic, simple supplication like that of a child that is fully aware of itself.

Every limitation opens up to an infinite reality. Thus you not only feel that you can do things once more, you want to do things. Mercy appears historically like the opposite of revolution in all its characteristics. Its essential and historical fruit in the person is called peace, the reconstruction of a subject in all its powers for a new work. The Prophet Isaiah said, "You are walking in the desert, but I have already built a new road, do not you see it?"[25] The desert is the image of someone who attempts revolution – this is the human pretension of pulverizing the endeavours produced by values acknowledged in previous ages. Although this pretension is destined to last but a few years, its direct, immediate effect is destructive. The new road is really made of mercy and peace – this is the finest definition of hope.

3   GOD IS LOVE – A POSITIVE HYPOTHESIS IN EVERYTHING

The point in which the Mystery reveals itself to us as mercy is a Man born of woman, who shatters all the limited images and plans that we can form with our imagination. This is why when they saw Him acting and speaking, they approved of Him. This man is Jesus. Jesus's revelation, that God is love, that God's nature is love,[26] means that the aim of everything that exists is absolutely positive.

It is certain that God cannot reduce to nothing even one good work – even one – done by man. For if the nature of being is love, then even a single good action can defend whole lives. This is the strange dimension that the word mercy brought into the realm of the word forgiveness, as an answer that to us seems "irrational" or "unjust," because it doesn't seem to have sufficient reasons. But the Mystery surpasses our measure. It is based on the gap between what man is and his action, between the conceivable and the objective terms of his action. Only the Mystery can span this disproportion. In Sigrid Undset's novel, Kristin Lavransdatter grasped this well, at the end of her life, this luminous positivity of life at its origin:

> And the last clear thought that formed in her brain was that she should die ere this mark had time to vanish – and she was glad. It seemed to her to be a mystery that she could not fathom [this is what we called 'irrational' or 'unjust'], but which she knew most surely none the less, that God had held her fast in a covenant made for her without her knowledge by a love poured out upon her richly – and in despite of her self-will, in despite of her heavy, earthbound spirit, somewhat of this love had become part of her, had wrought in her [it is St Peter's *yes*] like sunlight on the earth, had brought forth increase which not even the hottest flames of fleshly love nor its wildest bursts of wrath could lay waste wholly. A handmaiden of God she had been – a wayward, unruly servant, oftenest an eye-servant in her prayers and faithless in her heart, slothful and neglectful, impatient under correction, but little constant in her deeds – yet had he held her fast in his service.[27]

The book of Wisdom already reflected this positivity, "God did not make death, and He does not delight in the death of the living. For He created all things that they might exist, and the generative forces of the world are wholesome, and there is no destructive poison in them; and the dominion of Hades is not on earth. For righteousness is immortal. But ungodly men by their words and deeds summoned death."[28] A total positivity in life must guide the soul of the Christian, in whatever situation it is, whatever remorse it might feel,[29] whatever injustice it may feel weighing upon it, whatever darkness or enmity surrounds it, whatever death assails it, because God, who made all beings, is for the good. God is the positive hypothesis on all that man lives, even though this positivity seems at times to be overcome in us by the storms of life, almost as if leaving space for a capacity that man has for hostility, for hatred towards God's faithfulness.

"Rejoice with Jerusalem, and be glad for her, all you who love her; rejoice with her in joy, all you who mourn over her; that you may suck and be satisfied with her consoling breasts; that you may drink deeply with delight from the abundance of her glory. For thus says the LORD: 'Behold, I will extend prosperity to her like a river, and the wealth of the nations like an overflowing stream; and you shall suck, you shall be carried upon her hip, and dandled upon her knees. As one whom his mother comforts, so I will comfort you; you shall be comforted in Jerusalem. You shall see, and your heart shall rejoice; your bones shall flourish like the grass.'"[30]

And Psalm 77 says, "Our fathers went on sinning and had no faith in his wonders; so he ended their days like a breath and their years in sudden ruin. When he slew them then they would seek him, return and seek him in earnest. They would remember that God was their rock, God the Most High their redeemer. But the words they spoke were mere flattery; they lied to him with their lips, For their hearts were not truly with him; they were not faithful to his covenant. Yet he who is full of compassion forgave their sin and spared them. So often he held back his anger when he might have stirred up his rage. He remembered that they were only men, a breath that passes never to return."[31]

One of the greatest, really diabolical, sins that man can commit, for any reason at all (because of his sins, because he is unable to do the good that he desires, to repair the breaches made in the wall of his buildings by time and by circumstances), is to lose trust in God. God, as mercy, is victorious over everything. Certainly, a Christian must accept this victory. To live love, there is no need to make a list of virtues and perfections. In spite of what you are, you must accept the plan of an Other, you must be disposed to the will of God. This is man's vocation. "Vocation is the star that shines in the dark night of circumstances."[32]

"You give the Church of Christ to celebrate unutterable mysteries in which our human misery of mortal creatures is exalted in an eternal relationship; and our existence in time begins to blossom in eternal life. So, following your loving plan, man passes from a mortal condition to a wondrous salvation."[33] Gladness is the gift of the fatherland, while mercy is the peace of the journey. "Come, Lord Jesus!"[34]

...

Notes

CHAPTER ONE

1 See L. Giussani, *Il valore di alcune parole che segnano il cammino cristiano*, in "L'Osservatore Romano," 6 April 1996, 4.

2 F. Mauriac, *Life of Jesus*. Julie Kernan, trans. (New York: Longmans, Green and Co. 1937).

3 John 1:14.

4 See L. Giussani, *Il tempo e il tempio. Dio e l'uomo* (Milan: BUR 1995), 43–6; see also L. Giussani *At the Origin of the Christian Claim*, Viviane Hewitt, trans. (Montreal: McGill-Queen's University Press 1998), 44–5.

5 John 1:35–6.

6 See Matthew 3:1–6; Mark 1:4–8; Luke 3:7–18.

7 John 1:29.

8 John 1:37–9.

9 John 1:39.

10 See John 1:40–1.

11 John 1:42.

12 John 1:43.

13 See Luke 2:36–8.

14 See Luke 2:25–35.

15 See Luke 2: 8–20.

16 See L. Giussani, *At the Origin*, 100–4.

17 Dante Alighieri, *Paradise*, The Rev. H.F. Cary, trans. (London: William Smith 1845), XXIII, 104–5.

18 See L. Giussani, *At the Origin*, 29–35.

19 Isaiah 48:6–7.

20 2 Peter 1:4.

21 See Marius Victorinus, "In Epistola ad Ephesios," Liber secundus, in *Marii Victorini Opera exegetica,* cap. 4, 14.

22 A. Camus, *Notebooks 1935–1959* (New York: Marlowe 1998).

23 See the three methodological premises (Realism, Reasonableness, and Morality of Cognition), in L. Giussani *The Religious Sense,* John Zucchi, trans. (Montreal: McGill-Queen's University Press 1998), 3–33.

24 A. Finkielkraut, "Tirerò Péguy fuori dal ghetto" (*I Will Pull Péguy out of the Ghetto*). Interview with S.M. Paci, in *30 Giorni* (6), June 1992.

25 C. Pavese, *Il mestiere di vivere,* (*The art of living*) (Torino: Einaudi 1952), 14.

26 See I. de la Potterie, "Guardare per credere." Interview with A. Socci, in *Il Sabato* (46), 14 November 1992, 60–5.

27 See A.M. Severinus Boethius, *De consolatione philosophiae,* V, prose 1,12–19. See Aristotle, *Physica* II, 4–5 and *Ethica Nic.* III, 5.

28 A.M. Severinus Boethius, *De consolatione philosophiae,* V, prose 1,12–19.

29 See L. Giussani, *The Religious Sense,* 100–9.

30 See Matthew 6:25–34.

31 See L. Giussani, *Why the Church?,* Viviane Hewitt, trans. (Montreal: McGill-Queen's University Press 2001), 222.

32 See Colossians 1:17.

33 About the reductions effected by modernity, see *Tu o dell'amicizia.* Notes from meditations by Luigi Giussani and Stefano Alberto. Supplement to *Litterae Communionis-Tracce* (6), 1997. 5ff. and 14ff. See also *The Miracle of a Change.* Notes from meditations by Luigi Giussani, Rimini 1998, 14–23.

34 See L. Giussani, *The Religious Sense,* 35–40.

35 L. Giussani, *The Religious Sense,* 57.

36 L. Giussani, *The Religious Sense,* 99.

37 See L. Giussani, *At the Origin,* 12–13.

38 L. Giussani, *At the Origin,* 21–8.

39 John 14:6.

40 See Luke 2:1–7.

41 John 10:30.

42 John 15:5.

43 See John 10:15–16; 31–8.

44 See L. Giussani, *Why the Church?*, 14–17.

45 See L. Giussani, *Tracce di esperienza cristiana* (Milano: Jaca Book 1991), 29–39; 67–85.

46 See Luke 10:1–16; see also L. Giussani, *Why the Church?*, 20–3.

47 See Luke 10:17.

48 Mark 1:15.

49 See L. Giussani, *Why the Church?*, 88–90.

50 John 1:42.

51 See L. Giussani, *Is It Possible to Live This Way? Vol. 1, Faith* (Montreal & Kingston: McGill-Queen's University Press 2008), 16–32; 45–8.

52 Luke 19:1–10.

53 See Luke 7:11–17.

54 See John 9:13–34.

55 See L. Giussani, *The Religious Sense*, 27–33; 125–8.

56 See L. Giussani, *Tracce di esperienza cristiana*, 80–4.

57 See John 4:5–30.

58 See Matthew 16:17.

59 See Genesis 2:19–20.

60 Matthew 11:25.

61 See Colossians 1:17.

62 See *The Miracle of a Change*. Notes from meditations by Luigi Giussani, 29.

63 John 6:60ff.

64 John 4:1–42.

65 Faith is the recognition that God became a factor of present experience, the recognition of God present in time. As He happens in the present, God changes the circumstances of time and space. *Capable of changing time*: this is the supreme Christian statement, which in Catholicism, as opposed to Luther, wholly manifests its integrity. In the whole history of the Church the most painful thing is that Luther, to give everything to Christ, denied Him the capacity to change us in a real way. On the contrary, Christ changes

us precisely by saving the fragility and appearance of reality, which consists of Him dead and risen. According to Luther the affirmed centrality and totality of Christ, His strength as a Redeemer, remain in a way external to reality, that is, marked by contradiction and negativity beyond repair.

66 Revelation 22:17.

67 See Mark 4:41; Matthew 8:27.

68 "But perhaps there is one who listens to me, one who sees me / invisible ... / Who are you, whom I do not see, / who see me, speak then, where am I?" G. Pascoli, "Il cieco," in *Poesie* (Milano: Garzanti 1994), 335–6.

69 John 4:1–26; 9:1–38.

70 Luke 19:1–10.

71 Matthew 16:16.

72 Matthew 16:23.

73 John 21:15–19.

74 See L. Giussani, *Alla ricerca del volto umano* (Milano: Rizzoli 1995), 87–9.

75 John 1:41.

76 See Isaiah 49:6.

77 See Luke 24:13–35.

78 "Shower, O heavens, from above, and let the skies rain down righteousness" (Isaiah 45:8).

79 See Letter of the Church of Smyrna on the Martyrdom of St Polycarp. Funk, *Patres Apost.*, 1:297–9.

80 Hebrews 13:8.

81 See L. Giussani, *Is It Possible to Live This Way? Vol. 2, Hope* (Montreal & Kingston: McGill-Queen's University Press 2008), 87–9.

82 See Romans 12:1–2.

CHAPTER TWO

1 See L. Giussani, *Why the Church?*, Viviane Hewitt, trans. (Montreal: McGill-Queen's University Press 2001), 185, 189.

2 See Ephesians 1:23. See also L. Giussani, *Why the Church?* 118– 20.

3 See John 10:28–29. See also L. Giussani, *Why the Church?* 187–8.

4 Ephesians 4:13.

5 Acts 9:4.

6 See Luke 7:11–17.

7 John 11:25.

8 See John 14:6.

9 See John 1:35–39.

10 See Luke 19:5.

11 See Matthew 18:2–10.

12 See Matthew 9:36; Mark 6:34.

13 See Romans 6:4; Galatians 3:27.

14 Galatians 3:27–8.

15 See Romans 10:12; 1 Corinthians 12:13; Galatians 3:28; Colossians 13:11.

16 1 Corinthians 10:17.

17 See Ephesians 4:25.

18 John 10:30.

19 John 14:6.

20 See Ephesians 4:4–6; 11–25.

21 Colossians 3:11.

22 See "Etenim ille benedicendo vira omnes discipulis suis con-ferens, cum alia bona verbis illis, quibus ad Patrem utitur, tribuit dignis: tum edam addii hoc, quod bonorum caput ac summa est, non amplius eos in diversitate quadam electionum, multipliciter divisos fore in faciendo de bono judicio, sed omnes unum futuros, uni illi ac soli bono agglutinatos" (Gregory of Nyssa, *Homilies on the Song of Songs*, Hom. XV, PG 44,1115 D-1 118 A).

23 See Acts of the Apostles 9:26–29.

24 See John 10:23; Acts of the Apostles 3:11; 5:12.

25 Genesis 1:2.

26 See Acts of the Apostles 2:1–4; Ephesians 2:11–22; 1 Peter 2:10.

27 See Romans 12:4–5; 1 Corinthians 6:15; 12:12–27; Ephesians 4:25; 5:30.

28 See 1 Corinthians 15:28.

29 Colossians 3:11.

30 Colossians 1:17.

31 See Luigi Giussani, *Il tempo e il tempio. Dio e l'uomo* (Milan: BUR 1995), 13.

32 See Deuteronomy 7:7–9.

33 See Galatians 3:6–25; 1 Corinthians 10:1–13.

34 See John 5:19–21, 30.

35 See Acts of the Apostles 17:22ff.

36 See John 5:36; 6:57; 7:29; 8:42; 10:36; 11:42; 17:3–25; 20:21.

37 See Hebrews 3ff.

38 See John 8:25ff.

39 John 5:17, 19, 30, 36–7.

40 John 6:38–9, 44.

41 John 7:16, 28.

42 John 8:16, 26, 28–9.

43 John 13:3.

44 John 14:7, 9, 20, 31.

45 John 15:15, 24.

46 John 16:15, 28, 32.

47 John 17:1–2, 6–7, 10, 18, 25–6.

48 See L. Giussani, *Il tempo e il tempio*, 15ff.

49 See Luke 1:26–56.

50 See Romans 1:8; Philippians 1:5; Colossians 1:6; 1 Thessalonians 1:8.

51 See L. Giussani, *Alla ricerca del volto umano* (Milano: Rizzoli 1995), 80.

52 See L. Giussani, *Why the Church?*, 164–79.

53 Ibid., 179–200.

54 Ibid., 222–3.

55 Ibid., 117–20; 124–8. See also L. Giussani, Alla picerca del volto umano, 163–87.

56 See Matthew 19:26; Mark 10:27; Luke 18:27.

57 See 1 Timothy 2:4.

58 Acts of the Apostles 10:40–42.

59 See Exodus 23:10–11; Leviticus 25:1–7, 18, 22; 26:34–5, 43; 2 Chronicles 36:21; 1 Maccabees 6:49, 53–4.

60 John 17:1–2.

61 John 15:14–16.

62 Mark 3:13–19.

63 See *Il Senso di Dio e l'uomo moderno* (Milano: BUR 1994), 65–6.

64 See John 17:2.

65 Galatians 3: 26–7.

66 See Exodus 15:3.

67 Paul VI, General Audience, 23 July 1975, reported in "L'Osservatore Romano" 25 July 1975.

68 See Galatians 3:27.

69 Galatians 3:27–8.

70 See Romans 12:5; Ephesians 4:25.

71 See John 17:1ff; Colossians 1:17.

72 See L. Giussani, *Why the Church?*, 188.

73 See 2 Corinthians 5:17; Galatians 6:15.

74 2 Corinthians 5:17.

75 Galatians 6:15.

76 Colossians 3:9–10.

77 Ephesians 4:23–4.

78 See James 1:18.

79 1 Peter 1:23.

80 John 17:9.

81 See L. Mortari (ed.), *Vita e detti dei Padri del deserto* (Roma: Città Nuova 1971), I, 90.

82 1 John 5:4.

83 John Paul II, Discourse on the occasion of the thirtieth anniversary of Communion and Liberation, Rome, 29 September 1984.

84 John 1:18.

85 See John 3:1–21.

86 "Le plus grand des élèves, s'il est seulement élève, s'il répète seulement, s'il ne fait que répéter, je n'ose pas même dire la même résonance, car alors ce n'est plus même une résonance, pas même un écho, c'est un misérable décalque, le plus grand des élèves, s'il n'est qu'élève, ne compte pas, ne signifie absolument plus rien, éternellement est nul. Un élève ne vaut, ne commence a compter que au sens et dans la mesure où lui-même il introduit une voix, une résonance nouvelle, c'est-à-dire très précisément au sens et dans la mesure même où il n'est plus, où il n'est pas un élève. Non qu'il n'ait pas le droit de descendre d'une autre philosophie et d'un autre philosophe. Mais il en doit descendre par les voies naturelles de la filiation, et non par les voies scolaires de l'élevage" (Charles Péguy, *Cahiers,* VIII, XI [3.2.1907]).

87 John 15:13.

88 See 1 Corinthians 10:31.

89 See R. Guardini, *L'essenza del Cristianesimo* (Brescia: Morcelliana 1980), 12. Original Edition, *Das wesen des christentums* (Würzburg: Werkbund-verlag 1938).

90 See Luke 2:35.

91 Galatians 2:20.

92 Matthew 10:30.

93 See Matthew 12:36.

94 See L. Giussani, *Vivendo nella carne* (Milano: BUR 1998).

95 See L. Giussani, *The Religious Sense,* John Zucchi, trans. (Montreal: McGill-Queen's University Press 1998), 100–9.

96 See Galatians 2:20.

97 See Colossians 1:17.

98 Luke 18:9–14.

99 See Luke 18:13.

100 Psalm 62:12.

101 See Romans 14:10–13.

102 See 1 Corinthians 4:3.

103 Luke 23:34.

104 See John 1:42.

105 1 John 3:3.

106 John 17:3.

107 In this regard a quotation from St Ambrose can help. In his long comment on the Creation, when he reaches the seventh day, the day God rested, he affirms, "I thank the Lord our God who created such a marvellous work in which to find his rest. He created heaven, and I don't read that he rested; he created the earth, and I don't read that he rested; he created the sun, the moon, the stars, and I don't read that he rested even then; but I read that he created man and at this point he rested, having a being whose sins he could forgive" (St Ambrose, *Exameron*, IX, 76, in *Opera omnia di Sant'Ambrogio,* Vol. 1, Biblioteca Ambrosiana-Città Nuova Editrice, Milano-Roma 1979, 419).

108 See O. Milosz, *Miguel Manara* (Milano: Jaca Book 1998), 48–63.

109 Preface of XVI Sunday of Ordinary time.

110 Letter to Diognetus, *Migne* PG 2, 1167–86.

111 See St Thomas, *Summa Theologiae*, II, IIae, q. 179, art. 1.

112 See John 21:20–2.

113 *Jesu, tibi vivo*, Mediaeval hymn (Jesus, yours I live, Jesus, yours I die. Jesus, whether I live or die, I am yours).

114 1 John 4:8.

115 See Luke 19:1–10.

116 See 2 Corinthians 3:18.

117 See Romans 8:19–23.

118 Péguy wrote some wonderful pages about freedom. See for example *The Mystery of the Holy Innocents*, Pansy Pakenham, trans.; introduction by Alexander Dru (New York: Harper c1956).

119 See Luke 18:9–14.

120 See John 21:15–19.

121 John 1:40–2.

122 See Matthew 12:1–14; 15:1–20.

123 See John 6:68.

124 See Matthew 16:21–3.

125 V. Alfieri, "Lettera responsiva a Ranieri de' Casalbigi [6 September 1783]," in *Tragedie*, I, Paris 1888, p. LXXX.

126 See the final words of the dramatic poem by H. Ibsen, *Brand*. "Answer me, O God above! In death's jaws: Can human will, summed, avail no fraction of salvation?" Henry Ibsen, *Brand: A Dramatic Poem*, F.E. Garrett, trans. (London & Toronto: J.M. Dent & Sons 1917), 223.

127 See L. Giussani, *At the Origin of the Christian Claim*, Viviane Hewitt, trans. (Montreal: McGill-Queen's University Press 1998), 48–58.

128 1 Kings 19:11–12.

129 Psalm 63(62):9.

130 See L. Giussani, *The Religious Sense*, 145.

131 See Exodus 33:11, 15, 18. See also L. Giussani, *At the Origin*, 19–20.

132 See Colossians 3:11.

133 See L. Giussani, *Il tempo e il tempio*, 19–20.

134 See 1 Peter 2:5.

135 "Christe cunctorum dominator alme," Hymn for the dedication of a Church, in *Analecta Hymnica Medii Aevi*, Vol. 27, C. Blume, ed. (Leipzig 1897), 265.

136 Colossians 1:17.

137 The *Memores Domini* are those who live dedication to Christ
and to the Church in virginity. This experience was born from
the movement Communion and Liberation. The Association
Memores Domini (commonly called "Gruppo Adulto") means to
be a missionary presence through the form of virginity to bring
faith into men's lives, by meeting them everywhere, in particular
in the various work environments: school, office, factory. The
Memores Domini normally live together in a "house," in a fixed
community of from three to twelve.

138 The *Fraternity of Communion and Liberation* is a Public
Association of the Faithful, recognized by the Pontifical Council
for the Laity, 11 February 1982.

139 "O domus luminosa et speciosa, dilexi decorem tuum, et lo-
cum habitationis gloriae Domini mei, fabricatoris et posses-
soris tui. Tibi suspiret peregrinatìo mea, et dico ei qui fecit te,
ut possideat et me in te, quia fecit et me … Hierusalem domus
Dei aeterna, non obliuiscatur tui anima mea: post Christi dilec-
tionem tu sis laetitia mea: dulcis memoria beati nominis tui sit
releuatio moeroris et taedii mei." John of Fécamp, "Confessio
theologica" 23, 39, in *Pregare nel Medioevo* (Milano: Jaca Book
1986), 241–2.

140 "Hujus autem unitatis nexus est gloria" (Gregory of Nyssa,
Homilies on the Song of Songs, Hom XV, *Migne*, PG 44, 1118 A).

141 Isaiah 58:12.

142 Matthew 9:36.

143 See Dionisius the Areopagite, *De divinis Nominibus* 953 A 10.

144 See L. Giussani, "Communion and Liberation: an exemplary
method of education and a Christian anthropology," in *Alla ricerca del volto umano. Contributo ad un'antropologia* (Milano: Jaca
Book 1984), 87–103.

145 Joseph Ratzinger, *Presentation of the Catechism of the Catholic
Church*, in "L'Osservatore Romano," 20 January 1993, 5.

146 See John 3:8.

147 See Matthew 28:20.

148 See L. Giussani, *Is It Possible to Live This Way, Vol. 3, Charity*
(Montreal: McGill-Queen's University Press 2009), 81–5.

149 See John Paul II, *Be the teachers of Christian culture*, to the priests of Communion and Liberation, 12 September 1985. See also John Paul II, *The Importance of Charisms in the Church*, Meeting with Ecclesial Movements and New Communities, Rome, 30 May 1998.

150 See John Paul II, *Be the teachers*.

151 See John Paul II, *Spread the joy of the encounter with Christ*, to the members of the Pontifical Council for the Laity, Rocca di Papa, 14 March 1992.

152 See L. Giussani, "Il 'potere' del laico, cioè del cristiano," in *Un avvenimento di vita cioè una storia* (Roma: Edit-Il Sabato 1993), 53.

153 A.M. Cocagnac, "Chant de penitence," in the Songbook of Communion and Liberation.

154 See Matthew 3:9.

155 1 Corinthians 1:26–31.

156 James 2:12–13.

157 L. Giussani, *Is It Possible to Live This Way, Vol. 3*, 81–5.

CHAPTER THREE

1 "Populus est coetus multitudinis rationalis rerum quas diligit concordi communione sociatus, profecto, ut videatur qualis quisque populus sit, illa sunt intuenda quae diligit" (Saint Augustine, *De Civitate Dei* XIX, 24).

2 Exodus 12–15.

3 See Genesis 12:1–9; 15; 22:15–18.

4 See Matthew 1:1–17.

5 See John 10:23; Acts of the Apostles 3:11; 5:12.

6 Acts of the Apostles 15:14–18; see Amos 9:11–12.

7 See L. Giussani, *Why the Church,?* Viviane Hewitt, trans. (Montreal: McGill-Queen's University Press 2001), 91–8.

8 See C. Péguy, *The Mystery of the Holy Innocents*, Pansy Pakenham, trans.; introduction by Alexander Dru (New York: Harper c1956).

9 See L. Giussani, *Why the Church?*, 66–71.

10 See John 21:15–17.

11 See Matthew 16, 17–19.

12 Matthew 9:36.

13 See O.W. Milosz, "Miguel Manara, A Mystery in Six Scenes." Edward J. O'Brien, trans. In *Poet Lore: A Magazine of Letters* 1919 (summer), 247.

14 1 John 3:3.

15 See John 20:3–10.

16 Galatians 3:27–28; see Romans 10:12; 1 Corinthians 12:13; Colossians 3:11; see also L. Giussani, *Why the Church?*, 119–22.

17 See John 17:21.

18 J.H. Newman, *The Arians of the Fourth Century* (London: Longmans Green & Co 1908), 257.

19 See 2 Corinthians 5:6–9.

20 T.S. Eliot, *Choruses from "The Rock,"* in *Collected Poems 1909–1962* (London: Faber and Faber 1974), 178.

21 See John 15:18.

22 See L. Giussani, *"Tu" (o dell'amicizia)* (Milano: BUR 1997).

23 A. MacIntyre, *After Virtue: a Study in Moral Theory* (London: Duckworth 1981), 244–5.

24 John 17:2.

25 See Psalm 32(31); 131(130):2.

26 1 Corinthians 15:28.

27 T.S. Eliot, *Choruses from "The Rock,"* 168.

28 Ibid., 175.

29 See John 16:33.

30 Matthew 24:36.

31 "*Qui est* ... significat enim esse in praesenti: et hoc maxime proprie de Deo dicitur, cuius esse non novit praeteritum vel futurum, ut dicit Augustinus in *5 De Trinit.*" (St Thomas, *Summa Theologiae*, q. 13, art. IIe).

32 Antiphon at the Breaking of Bread, Ambrosian liturgy, III Sunday of Advent. See Isaiah 30:19–20.

33 John 15:11.

34 1 Corinthians 2:1–2.

35 1 Corinthians 15:28.

36 See Colossians 1:24.

37 T.S. Eliot, *Choruses from "The Rock,"* 177.

38 James 3:16; 4:1–4.

39 T.S Eliot, *Choruses from "The Rock,"* 177–8.

40 See C. Péguy, *Veronica. Dialogo della storia con l'anima carnale* (Lecce: Milella 1994), 144. Original edition *Veronique, Dialogue de l'histoire et de l'âme charnelle* (Paris: Gallimard 1972).

41 See John 11:46.

42 Paul VI, in "L'Osservatore Romano," 25 July 1975.

43 J. Guitton, *Paolo VI segreto* (Milano: Edizioni Paoline 1985), 152–3.

44 Tomas Luis de Victoria, "Eram quasi agnus" in *Tenebrae Responsoria* from the office of Holy Week.

45 See John 15:18–27.

46 See particularly John 8:44.

47 See Romans 13:1ff.

48 See John 15:18.

49 Nehemiah 8:1–11.

50 John Paul II, *Evangelium vitae*, 1, 105.

51 L. Giussani, *Why the Church?*, 183–9.

52 C. Dawson, *Religion and the Rise of Western Culture* (New York: Image 1958), 53–4. (Original edition, London: Sheed & Ward 1950).

53 See Galatians 2:20; Philippians 1:21; Colossians 3:34; Romans 8:35–39.

54 John 20:21; see John 17:18.

55 Galatians 4:6; Romans 8:15.

56 See Matthew 6:10.

57 John 17:1.

58 See *The Way of a Pilgrim*, a nineteenth century Russian story of a pilgrim who learns to recite the "Jesus prayer" ("Lord Jesus Christ, Son of God, have mercy on me a sinner") over and over again, a thousand times a day.

59 See Philippians 2:5–11.

60 2 Corinthians 5:14–15.

61 See Galatians 2:20.

62 See L. Giussani, *Is It Possible to Live This Way? Vol. 1, Faith* (Montreal & Kingston: McGill-Queen's University Press 2008), 108–15.

63 See Galatians 2:20.

64 See Acts of the Apostles 3:13–16.

65 Eucharistic Prayer IV, Missal of the Ambrosian Rite.

66 See Ephesians 4:20; 5:2.

67 See Galatians 3:27–28; Romans 10:12; 1 Corinthians 12:13; Colossians 3:11.

68 1 Corinthians 12:12–27.

69 Dante Alighieri, *Paradise*, The Rev. H.F. Cary, trans. (London: William Smith 1845), XXIV, 89–91.

70 J. Zvèrina, "*Letter to the Christians of the West*" in *L'esperienza della Chiesa*, (Milano: Jaca Book 1971), 177–8.

71 Romans 12:1.

72 See Philippians 4:8.

73 See Romans 12:2.

74 See John 3:17.

75 Romans 12:1.

76 See L. Giussani, *Alla ricerca del volto umano. Contributo ad un'antropologia* (Milano: Jaca Book 1984).

77 See L. Giussani "If I weren't yours, my Christ, I would be a finished creature" La Thuile, 17 August 1997, supplement to *Traces* (8) September 1997.

78 1 Thessalonians 5:21.

79 See *The Unwritten Gospel ... and Agrapha of Jesus*, R. Dunkerley, ed. (London: Allen and Unwin Ltd 1925), 84.

80 "Who could ever speak of Christ's own love for man, brimming over with peace," Dionisius the Areopagite, *De Divinis Nominibus* 953 A 10.

81 1 Peter 3:9.

82 Psalm 18(17):2.

83 Philippians 4:13.

84 See Isaiah 58:12.

85 See *The Imitation of Christ*, Books I, 3, 8.

86 Jacopone da Todi, "Cantico de la natività de Iesù Cristo," Lauda LXIV, in *Le Laude* (Firenze: Libreria Editrice Fiorentina 1989), 218.

87 Jacopone da Todi, "Como l'anima se lamenta con Dio de la carità superardente in lei infusa," Lauda XC, in *Le Laude,* 318.

88 See L. Giussani, *The Risk of Education* (New York: Crossroad 2001), 50–2.

89 See L. Giussani, *The Religious Sense,* John Zucchi, trans. (Montreal: McGill-Queen's University Press 1998), 12.

90 G. Leopardi, "Alla sua donna," in *Cara beltà* ... (Milano: BUR 1996), 53ff.

91 See 1 Corinthians 10:31.

92 "Ciascun confusamente un bene apprende / nel qual si quieti l'animo, e disira; / per che di giugner lui ciascun contende," Dante Alighieri, *Purgatorio*, Canto XVII, 127–9 (English edition, Oxford: Oxford University Press 2009).

93 See L. Giussani, *Is It Possible to Live This Way?*, Vol. 1, Faith (Montreal & Kingston: McGill-Queen's University Press 2007), 57–67.

94 See Matthew 19:10–12.

95 See St Augustine, *De peccatorum meritis et remissione et de baptismo parvulorum*, PL 44,167–171, in particular 170.

96 See St Francis of Assisi, *The Little Flowers of St Francis of Assisi* (New York: Random House 1998), chap. VIII.

97 G. Leopardi, "Il pensiero dominante," v. 143, in *Cara beltà* ..., 77ff.

98 See L. Giussani, *The Religious Sense*, 105.

99 See Matthew 5:36; 10:30; Luke 12:7; 21:18.

100 L. Giussani, *The Religious Sense*, 119ff; *Is It Possible to Live This Way? Vol. 1, Faith*, 45ff; *Si può (veramente?!) vivere così?* (Milano: BUR 1996), 183ff.

101 See Genesis 1:28. See also L. Giussani, *Why the Church?*, 218–19.

102 "In hoc aliquis percipit se animam habere et vivere et esse, quod percipit se sentire et intelligere et alia huiusmodi opera vitae exercere" (St Thomas, *Quaestiones Disputatae De Veritate*, q. X, art. 8, c). See also L. Giussani, *The Religious Sense*, 35.

103 Matthew 28:20; John 14:18, 21.

104 "Veritas est adaequatio intellectus ad rem" (St Thomas, *Quaestiones Disputatae De Anima* 111,1,1–2). See also *Summa Theologiae*, I, q. 16, artt. 1 and 2.

105 "Prudentia est recta ratio agibilium" (St Thomas, *Summa Theologiae*, II, IIae, q. 47, art. 8, c).

106 John Paul II, *True culture is human development, Address to men of culture*, Rio de Janeiro, Brazil, 1 July 1980.

107 See L. Giussani, *Realtà e giovinezza. La sfida*, (Torino: SEI 1995), 162–71; *The Risk of Education*, 7–27.

108 See Matthew 5:38.

109 John Paul II, *Dives in Misericordia*, 12.

110 Galatians 3:11. See Habakkuk 2:4; Romans 1:1–17.

111 See L. Giussani, "Il senso religioso, le opere, il potere," in *La politica per chi, per cosa,* suppl. a "Il Sabato" (22), 30 maggio 1987, 7–12.

112 See R. Guardini, *Power and Responsibility* (Chicago: Regnery 1961). Originally published as *Die Macht: Versuch einer Wegweisung* (Wurzburg: Werkbund 1951).

113 See *Gaudium et Spes,* 14, 2.

114 See John Paul II, *Dives in Misericordia,* 11.

115 See particularly P.P. Pasolini, *Scritti corsari* (Milano: Garzanti 1993), 23, 41, 45ff, 54.

116 A "loose, informal and open association of people" committed to human rights. Signatories included the playwriters Vaclav Havel (later president of the Czech Republic) and Pavel Kohout.

117 See V. Belohradsky (conversations with), *L'epoca degli ultimi uomini,* in "L'Altra Europa," (6), november-december 1986, 5ff.

118 G. Carducci, "Ripresa – Avanti! Avanti!," vv. 70–1, in *Poesie* (Milano: Garzanti 1982), 163.

119 "Populus Sion, ecce Dominus veniet ad salvandas gentes: et auditam faciet Dominus gloriam laudis suae in laetitia cordis vestry." Confractorium of the IV Sunday of Advent, in *Messale Ambrosiano. Dall'Avvento al Sabato Santo* (Milano 1942), 78. See also Isaiah 66:19; Ezekiel 39:21–29; Revelation 19:7; Psalm 16(15):10–11; 106(105):4–5; 1 Peter 1:6–9.

120 See "Domine Deus, in simplicitate cordis mei laetus obtuli universa: et populum tuum vidi cum ingenti gaudio tibi offerre donaria. Domine Deus, custodi hanc voluntatem cordis eorum" (Offertory prayer of the ancient liturgy of the feast of the Sacred Heart of Jesus, in *Messale Ambrosiano. Dalla Pasqua all'Avvento* (Milano 1942), 225. See also 1 Chronicles 29:17–18.

121 John 15:11.

CHAPTER FOUR

1 G. Pascoli, "I due orfani," in *Poesie* (Milano: Garzanti 1994), 355.

2 A. Negri, "Atto d'amore," in *Mia giovinezza,* (Milano: BUR 1995), 70.

3 See Matthew 24:36; Mark 13:32.

4 1 Corinthians 15:28; see Ephesians 4:6; Philippians 3:21; Colossians 3:11.

5 In this regard see Giosue Carducci's tragic poem: "We die to-morrow, as the lost and loved ones / Yesterday perished; out of all men's mem'ries / And all men's loving, shadow-like and fleeting' / We too shall vanish. / Yes, we must die, friends; and the earth, unceasing / Still in its labour, round the sun revolving. / Shall ev'ry instant send out lives in thousands, / Sparks evanescent; // Lives which in new loves passionate shall quiver, / Lives which in new wars conquering shall triumph, / And unto Gods new sing in grander chorus / Hymns of the future. // Nations unborn yet! in whose hands the beacon / Shall blaze resplendent, which from ours has fallen, / Ye too shall vanish, luminous battalions, / Into the endless. // Farewell, thou mother. Earth, of my brief musings. / And of my spirit fugitive! How much thou, / Eons-long whirling, round the sun shalt carry / Glory and sorrow! // Till the day comes, when, on the chilled equator, / Following vainly heat that is expir-ing. / Of Man's exhausted race survive one only / Man, and one woman. // Who stand forsaken on the ruin'd mountains, Mid the dead forests, pale, with glassy eyeballs. / Watching the sun's orb o'er the fearful icefields / Sink for the last time." G. Carducci, "On Monte Mario," vv. 21–48, in G.A. Green, *Italian Lyrists of Today: Translations from Contemporary Italian Poetry with Biographical Notices* (New York: MacMillan 1893), 78.

6 Rembrandt, *The Return of the Prodigal Son*, St Petersburg, Hermitage.

7 See Luke 15:11–32.

8 See Hosea 11:8. "How can I give you up, O E'phraim! How can I hand you over, O Israel! How can I make you like Admah! How can I treat you like Zeboi'im! My heart recoils within me, my com-passion grows warm and tender."

9 See John Paul II, *Dives in Misericordia*, 2.

10 Luke 23:34.

11 Luke 1:38.

12 See 2 Corinthians 5:14–15.

13 "All the past was present to him. All the present was to him present. / All the future, all the time to come was present to him. All eternity was present to him. / Together and separately. / He

saw everything in advance and everything at the same time. / He saw everything afterwards. / He saw everything beforehand. / He saw everything as it happened, he saw everything at that moment. / Everything was present to him in all eternity. / He knew about the money and the potter's field. / The thirty pieces of silver. / As he was the Son of God, Jesus knew all. / And the Saviour knew that, even though he gave himself up completely, / He was not saving that Judas, whom he loves. //

And it was then he knew infinite suffering. / It was then that he knew, it was then he learned, / it was then that he felt the infinite agony, / And cried out like a madman in his horrifying anguish / With a cry that caused Mary, who yet stood, to stagger. // And by the Father's mercy he died his human death." Charles Péguy, *The Mystery of the Charity of Joan of Arc*, Julien Green, trans. (London: Hollis and Carter 1950), 166–7.

14 1 John 4:16.

15 See Gen 4:1–16.

16 See Matthew 18:21–35; 20:13–16.

17 Colossians 3:15.

18 See John 8:44.

19 See St Francis de Sales, *Introduzione alla vita devota* (Milano: BUR 1986), 112. English edition, *Introduction to the Devout Life* (New York: Vintage Books 2002).

20 See Luke 5:4–11.

21 Job 1:21.

22 Luke 6:36; see Matthew 5:48; Ephesians 4:32.

23 See Hosea 11:4.

24 See Psalm 131(130); Isaiah 66:12–13.

25 See Hosea 11:4.

26 See 1 John 4:16.

27 S. Undset, *Kristin Lavransdatter, III The Cross* (New York: Vintage Books 1987), 401.

28 Wisdom 1:13–16.

29 See 1 Corinthians 4:3.

30 Isaiah 66:10–14.

31 Psalm 78(77):32–9.

32 *Graffiti*, in *Litterae Communionis-Tracce* (4), April 1996, 72.
33 Preface for the 19 Sunday of the year, in the Missal of the Ambrosian Rite.
34 Revelation 22:20.

Name Index

Subject Index